ANDY MCILREE

The Apostle Jude's Tripod

A Survey of the Man, Method and Message of the New Testament's Forgotten Book

HAYES
PRESS Christian Publisher

Contents

INTRODUCTION 1

1. SALUTATION: ON THE BASIS OF 'WHO?' 5

2. SALVATION: ON THE BASIS OF 'WHY?' 20

3. CONTENTION: ON THE BASIS OF 'HOW?' 40

4. CONDEMNATION: ON THE BASIS OF 'WHAT?' 49

5. REVELATION: ON THE BASIS OF 'WHEN?' 67

6. BENEDICTION: ON THE BASIS OF 'WHERE?' 83

7. DOXOLOGY: ON THE BASIS OF 'WHOM?' 96

REFERENCES 111

APPENDIX 1 – JUDE'S TRIPODS 115

APPENDIX 2 – THE CHARACTER OF FALSE MEN 117

WHAT THINK YE OF CHRIST? 119

ABOUT THE AUTHOR 121

ABOUT THE PUBLISHER 122

INTRODUCTION

As you pick up this study of Jude's letter, the first thing you will discover is that it is one of God's little books, and that He has much to say to us through it. We have no idea how long it took to write, but it can easily be read within five minutes. Even so, it spans eternity past and future, history and prophecy, blessing and judgement, past revelation and fresh revelation, things known and not known, heaven's glory and hell's grief. Like all Scripture, Jude's brief contribution confirms that even the shortest messages such as Obadiah, Philemon, two of John's letters, and now his own, have a God-given relevance for us in the present day. They are equally inspired as larger books, and equally relevant for:

- reproof – showing when we are off track;
- correction – helping us to get back on track;
- instruction – enabling us to keep on track.

Halfway through the Book of the Revelation, we will find God's final "little book," and it's interesting that He calls it a *biblaridion*, which literally means 'a little book', diminutive of *biblos* (from which we get our word Bible). Significantly, it had been opened, so that its message from God and its consequences would be revealed, and we expect a similar sense of purpose as we explore Jude's message from God and the Holy Spirit opens it for us. It bears the hallmark of being part of the divine Word, and we can safely enjoy it as being 'a little Bible.'

Jude, the Author

In attempting to decide which Jude was called by God and enabled by the Holy Spirit to write this short letter, we can do no more than appeal to Scripture for clarification. Each of them drew his name from the Hebrew name *Jehudah*, which means celebrated or praise, yet it has been translated into English as Judah, Judas, and Jude.

- Two are mentioned as Judah in the Old Testament genealogies recorded in Matthew 1:2, also Luke 3:30 and 33;
- Another two were disciples of Jesus: one was *"the son of James,"* though the King James Version calls him *"the brother of James"* (Lk.6:16). In both cases, the words in italics don't form part of the original text, which means this particular Judas was simply "of James";
- One was a "brother" of Jesus in Matthew 13:55 and Mark 6:3;
- One was Judas of Galilee, mentioned in Acts 5:37 with details of his mission and death;
- One lived in Damascus, and Ananias visited him after of Saul's conversion (Acts 9:11);
- One also was known as Barsabas in Acts 15:22.

Of all these, only two are possibilities: Judas the apostle in Luke 6:16 and Jude the Lord's brother, but the likelihood of the former being the son of James makes the latter more likely.

The First Recipients

Unlike most other New Testament letters, Jude gives no indication regarding where his was received. It may be that the churches in Judea, including Jerusalem, were reeling from the effects of false teachers, and so his balanced approach was one of reassuring the faithful and recovering the fallen, while rebuking the falsifiers.

His Approach

A careful reading of the letter's twenty-five verses will show the possibility of identifying an orderly and very inter-connected outline, which addresses the problem and affirms a pattern of renewal and rebuilding.

1. Salutation - On the basis of 'Who?'

2. Salvation - On the basis of 'Why?'

3. Contention - On the basis of 'How?'

4. Condemnation - On the basis of 'What?'

5. Revelation - On the basis of 'When?'

6. Benediction - On the basis of 'Where?'

We trust you will be blessed, as the Spirit of God leads us step-by-step through each section of this very important letter. It's only small, but our God is the God of small things.

* * *

GOD'S INFANT, BOY, AND MAN

Omnipotence was well-concealed within His Infanthood,
Yet, even then, in Infant form He was th'incarnate God
Whose tiny frame in secrecy was wrapped and shaped by Him,
With every attribute combined within His tiny form.

Omniscience was thinly veiled when as a Boy He shared
With Temple-teachers of the Law and found them unprepared;
For what He asked, and things revealed, surpassed their range of
thought,
And showed th'unlimited wealth of truth this unknown Boy had
brought.

But infancy and boyhood were forerunners of the Man
Who came to show the power and thought of God's eternal plan.
Through Him – in wisdom, righteousness, and in His holiness
Redemption's Man was made a curse for those He'd save and
bless.
(A. McIlree)

1. SALUTATION: ON THE BASIS OF 'WHO?'

"Jude, a bondservant of Jesus Christ, and brother of James, to those who are called, sanctified by God the Father, and preserved in Jesus Christ: Mercy, peace, and love be multiplied to you" (Jude vv.1,2).

* * *

Jude's letter might be short in its length, but it's definitely not short of teaching. He begins with a salutation and ends with a benediction, and it's enlightening to see how the close complements the opening. There is no clear way of knowing who his readers were, but they were under severe fire from false teachers who aimed to undermine them as believers. Isn't it strange that assembly life can be helped by those who are mining and hindered by those who are undermining? The sad thing is, that even the essential character of God and the gospel of God were under attack, and Jude wanted to write to them about things that belonged to what he called *"our common salvation."* He didn't mean that it was ordinary or mediocre. No, he was concerned about them not having real fellowship in the gospel, and not sharing it with each other as they should.

Can you imagine an assembly losing its way in the gospel? As we will find out from our study, their opposition was as serious, and as fundamental, as challenging the Lord's sovereignty and authority. No wonder Jude was concerned! He had learned the hard way: growing up as an unbeliever in the same home in Nazareth as the Saviour before trusting in Him after His death and resurrection;[1] but the good thing is, he learned. At least, when he was an unbeliever, he knew he was an unbeliever, not like the men he speaks about in his letter who pretended to be believers and *"crept in unnoticed"* to upset those who believed. We may not have had too much trouble like that over the years, but we still need to check the temperature and pulse of assemblies to see if we really are living in the safety and enjoyment of *"our common salvation."*

His Background

Some Christians face fiercest opposition inside their own homes, but who would have thought it would be like that for Christ? When He said, *"If they persecuted Me, they will also persecute you,"*[2] who would have imagined that "they" could ever apply to family members? However, unlikely as that may have seemed, it became crystal clear that He had the home in mind when He said, *"a man's enemies will be those of his own household."*[3] His words were a quotation from Micah 7:6 where the word "household" (Heb. *bayith*) can be translated as "house" or "family," as we find it three times in 1 Chronicles 13:14 – *"The ark of God remained with the family of Obed-Edom in his house three months. And the Lord blessed the house of Obed-Edom and all that he had."* How remarkable it is that saying it *"remained"* infers it was settled, as if wedded to that home for it normally belonged in the Most Holy Place of the Tabernacle – the symbol of Christ in glory. That's where it truly was at home, yet God gave honour and blessing by causing it to be revered by Obed-Edom and his family in their home.

If only the Lord Jesus Christ had been as welcomed in His earthly home, but the Son of God never sensed the acceptance that was given to the ark of God. His true home is on the throne of God where He *"ascended far above all the heavens,"*[4] yet He exchanged it and descended to live under the same roof of unbelieving brothers and sisters who didn't show Him the same reverence as their parents. Far from it!

Little is said of His childhood years, other than His visit to the temple as a twelve-year-old.[5] Perhaps, the contrast comes into sharper focus if we borrow Asaph's words in Psalm 50:20-21 – *"You sit and speak against your brother; you slander* [Heb. *dophiy*: push] *your own mother's son. These things you have done, and I kept silent; you thought that I was altogether like you; but I will rebuke you, and set them in order before your eyes."* Their hostile words were intended to have the same effect as those who urged one another to *"smite"*[6] Jeremiah with the tongue. How wrong they were in thinking of the One who came *"in the likeness of men"*[7] that this meant He was *"altogether like"* what they were. Nothing could have been farther from the truth. He never shared their critical spirit, their selfishness or their abusive way of thinking. Scripture says, *"who, when He was reviled, did not revile in return; when He suffered, He did not threaten,"*[8] and that included His home-life.

As co-equal with His Father in character, He kept silent just as God did in Asaph's Psalm. But He not only condemned their actions, He noted their attitude as they assumed the right to despise His Word (v.16), His own (v.20), and Himself (v.21). He kept silent as they voiced belittling thoughts of Him, yet He could see that they were as settled in their irreverence as Obed-Edom's family were in their reverence. He made this very point by saying, *"You sit,"* which is exactly the same in Hebrew as when the ark *"remained"* with Obed-Edom. They were settled in their scorn and abuse, just as many others would be during the later years of His homelessness when He had *"nowhere to lay His head."*[9]

G.K. Chesterton spoke about "the place where God was homeless and all men are at home,"[10] yet the Lord had come to help them see that *"every good gift and every perfect gift is from above,"*[11] even if His own brothers fanned the well-known question, *"Can anything good come out of Nazareth?"*[12] No matter how many had looked askance at Nazareth's reputation, it was the place where the *"Lord of glory"*[13] who *"made himself of no reputation"*[14] chose to spend His pre-ministry years. It was one thing for Solomon to ask the question, *"Will God indeed dwell on the earth? Behold, heaven and the heaven of heavens cannot contain You. How much less this temple which I have built!"*[15] If the Temple seemed too little, what then about God manifested in the flesh dwelling in despised Nazareth? Joseph and Mary's humble home was the first household in Israel that, spiritually speaking, was too small for the Lamb,[16] yet Jude would grow up in it and discover that this God had great purposes for him.

His Foreground

There is inescapable evidence, and no room for doubt, that a great work of God was done in the hearts of Mary and Joseph's four sons – James, Joses, Simon, and Judas – during the forty days between Calvary and being included in the one hundred and twenty who gathered in Acts 1:14-15 to wait for the coming of the Holy Spirit. How and when the change took place, we don't know, but change they most certainly did. Perhaps, somewhere in the darkness of Calvary's cross, they felt their own darkness; perhaps, during the earthquake, they also were shaken; and perhaps, when the tombs were opened, they began to sense their own spiritual awakening. What we do know is that the Lord Jesus Christ was seen after His resurrection *"by Cephas, then by the twelve. After that He was seen by over five hundred brethren at once"* and *"After that He was seen by James, then by all the apostles."*[17] The exalted Christ had come into their lives in a wonderful fulfilment of the ark's covenant blessing.

The opening words of his letter put this at the forefront of his relationship with his Lord and Saviour, and come to us as a sincere acknowledgement of two births: one, spiritual, that allowed him to be *"a bondservant of Jesus Christ"*; the other, natural, that allowed him to be a brother of James. We should note how carefully he identified himself and realise that he did it by the leading of the Holy Spirit, just as John did when graciously distinguishing that another Judas was *"not Iscariot."*[18] Jude, the writer, was none other than one of Jesus' brothers, all of whom were unbelievers during the Lord's time on earth. No doubt, he could look back on these unbelieving days when all four taunted Jesus by saying, *"Depart from here and go into Judea, that Your disciples also may see the works that You are doing. For no one does anything in secret while he himself seeks to be known openly. If You do these things, show Yourself to the world.*"[19]

Their comments were made in the hollowness of unbelief, and with the intended mockery that He should perform before a larger audience. Jesus knew that it would not be long until He was shown to the world in a very different way from what they meant, for His crucifixion would take place at the Passover of the following year. God's timing is always exact, as Acts 1:7 points out by referring to *"times or seasons"* which in Greek – *chronous ē kairous* – means indefinite periods of time or definite moments in time. Jesus knew this, but His brothers didn't; yet they decided to voice their advice. How right Paul was when he emphasised that Deity needed no advisors in eternity – *"For who has known the mind of the Lord? Or who has become His counsellor?"*[20] – yet His brothers offered theirs.

However, the cross so effectively had come in between and, rejoicing in his blood-bought forgiveness, Jude took his place as a bondservant. There was no familiarity in his opening remark. He could easily have said, "Jude, a brother of Jesus Christ and bondservant with James," but, like James in his letter, he owned the Lordship of the One they formerly spoke against and their transformation as servants of the King. James called Him *"our Lord Jesus Christ, the Lord of glory"*[21] – or, more accurately by removing the words in italics, "our Lord Jesus Christ of the glory." By saying this, James was not only convinced of the glory of the place from which his Saviour had come, and to which He had returned, he was thinking of the glory of the Person and of how that glory should radiate through "the faith" that we hold. It was this that

Jude made his aim by describing his servanthood with the Greek word *doulos*. He could have used other words, each with its own characteristics. For instance:

- *diakonos*: a deacon, a menial helper (Lk.22:27; Matt.23:11; 1 Tim.3:8);
- *hupēretēs*: an under-oarsman in the lowest tier of rowers where he would feel the sweat and the spit from those who rowed in the upper tiers (Jn 18:36; Acts 26:16; 1 Cor. 4:1);
- *leitourgos*: a Temple minister or worshipper. Hebrews 1:7 refers to angels who minister (*leitourgeō*) Godward, and in v.14 as they minister (*diakoneō*) manward. Hebrews 8:2 refers to the Lord as the Minister (*leitourgos*) of the sanctuary; and Acts 13:2 describes certain brethren as they ministered (*leitourgeō*) to the Lord.

Each of these is a fitting description of a servant of God, but the Spirit of God attached the word *doulos* to Jude to speak of one who is tied to the task like a slave and not loosed without his master's permission. This is illustrated in Matthew 21:2 by the donkey and colt that were *"tied"* (Gr. *deō*, the root of *doulos* – Dr Strong) and loosed by their owner who showed subjection to the Lordship of Christ when told, *"The Lord has need of them."* And the unbroken colt showed its submission by allowing the Lord to ride on it. The word *doulos* also is linked to the word *dei* from which we get our word *"must,"* and we see the Lord Jesus Christ as the exemplary *doulos* when He said, *"The Son of Man **must** suffer many things"*[22] and *"I **must** work the works of Him who sent Me."*[23]

Another interesting use of the word is associated with essential or "**must**-prayer". This time, the word is *deomai* – to beg or plead with binding prayer, and we find examples of this:

- **In the Lord** – *"But I have prayed for you ..."* (Lk.22:32);
- **In the early church** - *"And when they had prayed, the place ... was shaken"* (Acts 4:31);
- **In the apostle Paul** – *"As though God were pleading through us, we implore you"* (2 Cor.5:20).

We should pause here to ask ourselves how often we are conscious of striving with this degree of necessity and intensity in prayer, not only in our personal prayer lives but in church Prayer Meetings. Each of us will recall times in both when we sensed and felt the evidence of deeply burdened prayer, and it may be we recall them with a sense of the unusual – a 'once-in-a-blue-moon' experience! Crises of one sort or another have the tremendous ability to drive us to prayer with greater urgency and dependence, and we plead for those much-needed answers that will glorify God and bring relief to our spirits. But isn't it true that our 'normal' prayer times can be made up of what the late Guy Jarvie, missionary to Burma and India, called "hospital prayers"? Prayer lists, prayer boards, prayer guides all have their place for they cover many 'prayer-points' that are important, but when last were you shaken as a Christian, and how long is it since your church's Prayer Meeting *"was shaken"*?

The first step that the early Jerusalem church took was in what was described as *deēthentōn* – binding, must-prayer – and the whole church prayed with an intensity that came from being *tied* to the need for prayer (Acts 4:31). They were discovering that continuing steadfastly[24] didn't simply mean regularly or routinely, but actively and unitedly casting their burdens on the LORD or, as it can be translated, casting *"what He has given,"*[25] and waiting for Him to sustain them. If only we could be moved as they were! It was a God-given disturbance, a Spirit-led stirring. Greeks called it a *salos* from *saleuō*, which includes the thought of "waves."[26] Oh for prayer times that are out of the ordinary and make the right sort of waves! For those in the Jerusalem church, it meant three vital needs being fulfilled:

- They were filled with the Holy Spirit;
- They spoke the word of God with boldness;
- They were united in one heart and one soul.

The inescapable lesson is, that those who are tied to the Lord as *doulos*-servants will be tied to Him in *doulos* prayer. Others were - are we?

Bondservant *(doulos)* seen in:

- The Lord- Phil.2:7;
- The early churches - Jn 15:15; Rom.6:19; 1 Pet.2:16;
- Paul - Rom.1:1; 2 Cor.4:5; Gal.1:10.

Must *(dei)* seen in:

- The Lord - Acts 17:3; 1 Cor.15:25;
- The early churches - Acts 4:12; 5:29; Heb.11:6;
- Paul - Acts 9:6.

For Jude, being a bondservant (*doulos*) was the spiritual result of recognising Jesus Christ as Lord (*Kurios*), and we will see later how he applied this reasoning to his condemnation of false teachers who couldn't be servants since they didn't know the Lord.

His Tripods

As we go through Jude's short letter it will become very noticeable that, like a surveyor, he sets up a series of tripods, eighteen in total (see APPENDIX 1), as he navigates the rugged contours of the gathering he had in mind. He was about to address the ups and downs of their Christian experience knowing full well that, while they were in this world, but not of it,[27] there were evil men among them who were in the church, but not of it. With this in mind, he drew their attention to the first triplet through which he commended the believers and condemned the unbelievers.

Like all Scripture, his little letter may seem to take the proportions of a dagger rather than a sword, yet it was breathed out by God to let His flock know how lofty their place was in Christ, and to let the ungodly know how low a place they occupied without Him. According to the New King James Version, the three spiritual blessings were addressed to those who were *"called, sanctified ... and preserved,"* but this should read, as in most other translations, *"called, beloved ... and kept."*

Called

If anything should settle the believer's faith, and unsettle the unbeliever's faithlessness, it's the God-given assurance that all His children have been called. Paul believed this, Peter was equally convinced, and Jude held the same conviction. Rooted in the heart of God, and settled in electing grace, every believer's spiritual journey begins with a much-needed response to the call of God. The voice of the LORD is powerful[28] and, by the power of the living word of truth,[29] He penetrates the hearts of those who are weak[30] and dead,[31] enlightens those who were in darkness and turns them from being children of wrath to children of light.[32]

Jude knew that God's call is not a futile, empty sound. By using the word *klētos*, he assured them that it was an invitation and an appointment, and this was why Paul urged every believer to "see" their calling in 1 Corinthians 1:26. In fact, he wanted this so much that he wrote the word *blepete* in such a way that it meant they should keep looking at it. On top of this, Jude wrote this word for *"called"* as an adjective and plural, exactly the same as in Romans 1:7, and we may wonder why. Unlike its two neighbouring words, beloved and kept, which are verbs, it describes the plural nature of God's call, which is high and holy and heavenly.[33] We can well understand how these believers who heard Jude's first triplet would rejoice in their gain, and wonder how the unbelieving could not feel convicted about their loss.

Beloved

How wonderful to be at the centre of the love of God! With Jude's background, he valued being loved by Him and the word *agapao* is intentionally used to emphasise the depth of divine affection that lies, firstly, at the heart of God's call, and then at the heart of His keeping power. Paul made a different point in 1 Corinthians 1:2 when he wrote about believers being *"sanctified in Christ Jesus, called saints."* Once again, *"called"* describes those who are holy, and "*sanctified*" (Gr. *hagiazo*) refers to the permanence of His preservation.

Kept

With the call of God sending our appreciation back to a past and eternal sovereign choice, Jude then directs his readers and us to an eternal future. This doesn't mean that he overlooked their present struggles, but rather that the reality of what they were going through should be viewed in the light of the past reality of their calling and the future reality of being eternally secure. In the meantime, even when it is difficult for us to keep our eyes fixed on our calling, the One who called is guarding, watching, and keeping His eye on us, which is the meaning of the word *tēreō*.

With this in mind, the Christian faces every trial and sees them through the promises of God in which He says, "*I will guide you with My eye* [upon you, ESV]"[34] and that "*the eyes of the LORD are in every place, keeping watch.*"[35] In the comfort of these, and in the midst of all sorts of opposition, we also take heart from knowing that "*there is no creature hidden from His sight, but all things are naked and open to the eyes of Him to whom we must give account.*"[36] The dear folks who listened to Jude's opening sentence wouldn't fail to see that his first tripod was central to what he was saying to them on either side of it. On the one hand, the bondservant knew His Master well and had the right spiritual credentials to share this threefold assurance. On the other, they would see that it stood related to their present need, and so he opened up the scope of his second tripod.

Mercy, peace, and love

It's wonderful to know that our salvation brought the heart of God into our hearts and that, in His grace, He also shared His mercy, made peace and showed love through the cross. By grace, we have received what we didn't deserve, and in mercy He kept us from receiving what we did deserve. In effect, Jude was saying to them that whatever spiritual blessing came to them would be confirmed by whatever spiritual blessings came through them. In other words, mercy received would make them merciful; peace received would make them peaceable; and love received would make them loving. Even so, they would have to work at it together if they were to overcome the ravages of the onslaught they were enduring.

Yes, God is merciful on the basis of His righteousness, and our showing of mercy must be consistent with the basis of His righteousness. This will keep us from margins of tolerance and intolerance that call for unrighteousness; for example, with current departures from His Word to accommodate challenges made by modern standards of morality and immorality. Likewise, peace is not at all costs, but with honour. God, and the gospel of God, must be honoured and never compromised by mercy, peace and love that are not consistent with what He has already shown. This means that whatever is received through genuine repentance cannot be shown toward those whose sins cause no repentance. Only what is multiplied to us should be multiplied through us!

The Scriptures are a two-edged sword that need to be handled wisely, and it will become evident how righteously Jude applied it during the course of his letter, to those who were faithful, to those who had fallen, and to those who were false. In encouraging *"those who have obtained like precious faith with us by the righteousness of our God and Saviour Jesus Christ,"*[37] Paul would have comforted Jude's readers by saying that their trials were *"manifest evidence of the righteous judgement of God, that you may be counted worthy of the kingdom of God, for which you also suffer."*[38] At the same time, he would tell false teachers that, *"in accordance with your hardness and your impenitent heart you are treasuring up for yourself wrath in the day of wrath and revelation of the righteous judgement of God."*[39] It's the same sword from the same God used in the same righteousness, but with two distinct messages, and this is exactly what we will find as we let Jude continue to speak.

IN CONTRAST

Wise, even in His foolishness,
And strong the weakness of His hand;
An endless deep His shallowness;
So vast, the tiniest things He planned.

Robust, yet veiled in gentleness,
And very God while truly Man;
He measures, yet is measureless,
With light years dwarfed within His span.

The Highest, in His lowliness;
Still Holy, though made sin for us,
And heaven's Best in emptiness
Dies with earth's worst upon a cross.

Engulfed in darkness is the Light,
And Love encounters hatred's power.
Heaven's Life expires within earth's night:
The Eternal One endures 'the hour'.

The Victim is the Victor now,
The One who died forever lives.
We gave our wickedness to Him:
His gentleness to us He gives.
(A. McIlree)

2. SALVATION: ON THE BASIS OF 'WHY?'

"Beloved, while I was very diligent to write to you concerning our common salvation" (Jude v.3).

"We give thanks to God always for you all, making mention of you in our prayers, remembering without ceasing your work of faith, labour of love, and patience of hope in our Lord Jesus Christ in the sight of our God and Father, knowing, beloved brethren, your election by God. For our gospel did not come to you in word only, but also in power, and in the Holy Spirit and in much assurance, as you know what kind of men we were among you for your sake.

And you became followers of us and of the Lord, having received the word in much affliction, with joy of the Holy Spirit, so that you became examples to all in Macedonia and Achaia who believe. But as we have been approved by God to be entrusted with the gospel, even so we speak, not as pleasing men, but God who tests our hearts" (1 Thess.1:2-7; 2:4).

* * *

Jude's salutation was exactly what this gathering of troubled believers needed to hear. It was sincere and heart-warming, and worded in such a way that they were reassured about their standing with God. At the same time, it reinforced them in their struggle for it drew the real battle lines. They were up against ungodly men who knew nothing about being *"called, beloved, and preserved"* so it was impossible for *"mercy, peace, and love"* to be multiplied, since they had never received them through salvation.

As for the believers, having just learned that they were *"beloved"* by God, Jude immediately described them as his *"beloved"* ones and, to make sure they knew how much he meant it, he made it one of his tripods as verses 3, 17 and 20 clearly show. God knows, and so did Jude, that affection is the best ground for cultivating spiritual fellowship and for building spiritual stewardship. So they knew that urging them to *"contend ... remember"* and to *"keep building"* all flowed from loving encouragement and not mere man-management.

The churches had been infiltrated, and Jude was burdened. The ink of his salutation would hardly be dry on the page when he went on to let them know that he was *"very diligent to write ... concerning our common salvation,"* which means he was so earnest about it that he couldn't do it quickly enough. The New King James Version says that he wanted to write *"concerning"* this, while others simply say "of" or "about." Jude's actual word was *peri*, which literally means he wanted to go "all over" or "all around" the matter. Had he gone ahead, he may have produced something as long as Paul's letter to the Romans to define what they should enjoy in their *"common salvation,"* but his letter was never written. Instead, he became one of the men God moved to write what He wanted to say, and one page was enough.

Our Common Salvation

As far as Jude was concerned, he didn't change course by dropping his initial burden to focus on *"the faith."* On the contrary, he shows that what belongs to one belongs to the other and, by his own admission, they needed to hear something that would strengthen them in *"our common salvation."* Whatever he had intended to write must have been connected to glorifying the gospel of God, its content and convictions, by drawing their attention to His nature and attributes; the nature of the message and its doctrines. His delightful phrase, *koinēs hēmon sotērias*, means "our shared deliverance and safety," and emphasises the thought of having fellowship in our salvation, in our knowledge of God as Creator and Redeemer, and in our understanding of the gospel.

This means having communion that is based solely on the conviction truths of the gospel, and fellowship in communicating what is based on the content of the gospel. What a springboard this is into our understanding and enjoyment of all that we have in Christ! It's also a safeguard against neglecting what God has given us in salvation by focusing on truth relating to what He gives us in service. So the things that are "necessary" include the necessity of checking that what we share is truly "common" and held in the assurance of Christ-centred fellowship. How lovely it is that verse 3 flows so spontaneously from verses 1 and 2, with no possibility of being divorced from them. This means that our calling, being beloved, and preserved, along with God's mercy, peace and love are attached and never detached from *"contending earnestly."* Brothers and sisters, we are wonderfully blessed!

It all goes hand in hand and affects:

- Fellowship in the gospel (Phil.1:5) - **COMMUNION;**
- Furtherance of the gospel (Phil.1:12) - **COMMITMENT;**
- The faith of the gospel (Phil.1:27) - **CONVICTION.**

It also affects:

- Fellowship in the gospel (Phil.1:5) - **PARTNERSHIP IN PREACHING;**
- The sharing of your faith may become effective (Phlm.5,6) - **PARTNERSHIP IN FAITH.**

As believers, we do this by seeking to understand what God believes and by Spirit-led reasoning, while others deviate from it by delusion, distortion, and deceit. This protects us from the sort of tolerance Paul feared possible in Corinth: *"If he who comes preaches another Jesus whom we have not preached, or if you receive a different spirit which you have not received, or a different gospel which you have not accepted—you may well put up with it!"*[1] What a frightening departure from the truth!

- A different messenger - not a true servant;
- A different Jesus - not the true Saviour;
- A different spirit - not the true Spirit;
- A different gospel - not the true message.

The New Testament speaks of a day when *"the man of sin – the lawless one,"*[2] also called Antichrist,[3] will come, and two distinct warnings are given. The first is by Paul, that *"the mystery of lawlessness is already at work"*; and the second by John, regarding *"the spirit of the Antichrist, which you have heard was coming, and is now already in the world."* How true this was in their day, and Jude's letter was prompted by the same problem. Although far from the day of the Antichrist, the churches were under attack by men who were anti-Christ in both spirit and substance, yet they were shielded by two aspects of divine protection. Paul refers to these as, *"what is restraining"* and *"He who now restrains."*[4]

It's helpful to note that his first phrase, *to katechon*, is neuter, and the second, *ho katechōn*, is masculine. We would suggest that the latter is the Holy Spirit Himself, and the former consists of living members of the church, which is the body of Christ. As the salt of the earth, they have a restraining effect until the whole church is caught up to heaven at the coming of the Lord. The Spirit and His work can resist and overcome the spirit and work of those who are false teachers, and their end will be *"among those who perish, because they did not receive the love of the truth, that they might be saved."*[5] The great dividing line couldn't be clearer: truth is in Jesus. Those who are *"in Christ Jesus"* possess Him and *"the word of the truth,"* and the lost did not receive Him or *"the love of the truth."*

- Truth is in Jesus (Eph.4:21) - **THE SAVIOUR;**
- The word of the truth (Col.1:5) - **THE SAVED;**
- Disapproved concerning the faith (2 Tim.3:8) - **THE LOST.**

Having set us free, God leaves us free to preach the doctrines of God and the doctrines of grace, and nothing else. True freedom belongs to being anchored in the doctrines of *"the gospel of God …*

of Christ ... of His Son."[6] He has brought us into *"the glorious liberty of the children of God"*[7] and asks us to *"stand fast"* in it. It's the standing fast of a fixed position that resists any temptation to *"be entangled again with a yoke of bondage."*[8] It's the standing fast of a fixed understanding that doesn't stand for one point of view today and a different opinion tomorrow. He has said, *"I am the LORD, I do not change,"*[9] and we know that *"Jesus Christ is the same yesterday, today, and forever,"*[10] so the terms of the gospel can't change.

This is what makes *"sound doctrine"*[11] and *"sound words"*[12] sound, and they can never become unsound. They also shape sound preaching and sound preachers, yet it's well known that some say things, not only unadvisedly, but even *"speak wickedly for God, and talk deceitfully for Him."*[13] When the Lord Jesus Christ said, *"I am the light of the world,"* and later said of others, *"You are the light of the world,"* He did two remarkable things: He showed that our humanity would be elevated to proclaim the focus of Deity, and He conferred on His witnesses the greatest responsibility that had ever been granted to servants of God. In these two phrases He elevated our humanity and our responsibility, and in a lovely way humbled Himself by conveying such a mission from the infinite scope of His hands to the limited scope of ours. Isaiah's graphic picture of Him who *"measured the waters in the hollow of His hand, measured heaven with a span"*[14] emphasises the sheer impossibility of our hands ever being equal to His.

How well He knew that our hands, so incapable of tracking the dimensions of the galaxies, are equally incapable of tracing and gripping the doctrines of the gospel, yet He has called us to handle the only message that is capable of bringing men and women to experience the eternal dimensions of the *"new creation."* The honour was equally expressed when Paul took Isaiah's words – *"How beautiful ... are the feet of Him"*[15] – and, by the Spirit, said to us *"How beautiful are the feet of them."*[16]

The Kind of Preaching – the Content of the Message

1 Thessalonians 1:2-6 and 2:4 give a wonderful summary, for these verses cover the sower, the seed and the soil. Firstly, we are introduced to the trio who served together in the gospel of God, Paul, Silvanus and Timothy, whose satisfaction is summed up in their thanking, mentioning, remembering and knowing, which shows how conscious they were that the purpose of the gospel rests entirely on the sovereignty of God. As they thought of their brothers and sisters, they assured them that they were thankful, and able to mention and remember them before God in prayer, because they were convinced by the evidence of a work of Christ in their lives that they were among God's elect. How wonderful it is that those who are convinced they have known a work of grace also cause others to see the evidence in them that God had elected them.

So, firstly, Paul was in no doubt that the *purpose* of the gospel rests entirely on the sovereignty of God. Secondly, he was absolutely sure that the *produce* of the gospel came from the good soil of believing hearts whose commitment to the Lord Jesus was driven by the mainspring of faith, love and hope. Thirdly, we are presented with the all-important aspect of God's *pleasure* in the gospel, so we are left in no doubt that the purpose of this glorious message is that it was designed to produce and to please.

The faithful sower can be faithful to the soil only if he is faithful to the seed. Perhaps, there are times when lack of production results not from trying to sow in the wrong soil, but from attempting to sow with the wrong seed. Germination depends on putting the right seed into the right soil, so each sower should stand between two works of God when we take the gospel of God to sinners of the world. Tampering with the seed suggests that the sower knows better than the Saviour, and that the servant knows better than the Master. If we depend more on the inspiration of this seed there will be greater expectation of germination in the soil! This was the great thrill of those in Thessalonica, and it can be updated into our experience as we go with the gospel of God, to point sinners by the Spirit of God to the cross of the Christ of God.

This unites two correlated important features, the first of which is the kind of preaching and the content of the message. As we bow under the colossal thought of an electing God of all grace, it puts us into an arena where our recognition of Him allows us to approach sinners confident that the God of heaven has a plan in view, and we are only a small part of it. But it's in this smallness that we trust His greatness and pray, as others have, "Lord, lead us to the elect." What a confidence. Election is not a shackle to the gospel; it's a spur. It nerves us for the gospel that we know the Saviour has sheep still to be gathered in, and we are among the messengers who handle such a glorious message.

When Paul said, *"our gospel did not come to you in word only,"*[17] this should ring an alarm bell in our hearts for it raises the possibility of preaching to men and women in an ineffective manner, because it's in word only. If the apostle Paul knew the need to safeguard his ministry from such a pit, then, God helping us, we will endeavour to do the same. He was so concerned about this that he didn't only drive his message home to the church in Thessalonica; he did it twice to the Corinthians, and said it again to all the churches of Galatia. It wasn't in the wisdom of words, nor was it with persuasive words. It didn't depend on his intellect, on his ability or on the vehicle of his mentality to make the message convincing. His fear was that, if that's the basis of the gospel, then the cross of Christ could *"be made of no effect."*[18] He feared the presentation of an ineffective Calvary, not because of Christ, but because of the kind of preaching. Can you imagine gospel preaching that leaves the cross having no effect on some listeners? Paul could! Fearful, isn't it?

Listen closely to the burdened apostle: *"Do I now persuade men or God? Or do I speak to please men? For if I still pleased men, I would not be a bondservant of Christ."*[19] This is the high price of inadequate content in the gospel: it fails to keep the preacher true to the Christ of the cross, and it fails to make the hearer true to the cross of Christ. If we fail in these, He will use another messenger. Is it the favour of men we are seeking to win or of God? Or is it men we are seeking to please, rather than Him? People-pleasing and playing to the gallery are roommates of what Job called *"speaking unrighteously for God."*[20]

Sadly, there's no shortage of this in today's range of preachers and preaching. God has put into our hands a message we should prize so fully that we will never be satisfied by sharing less than He has given. This doesn't conflict with Paul's comment about becoming *"all things to all men"*[21] for he had no intention of conflicting with the will of God or the doctrine of the Lord. He was sensitive to customs and circumstances, but he never became a weathervane pointing in all directions or pointing people in directions they'd later discover didn't comply with God's Word.

Methods can undermine the message, therefore we need to follow Paul's approach. Having spoken of the *purpose, produce and pleasure* of God in the gospel, he now speaks of its *power*. Only Spirit-led preaching is *"in power"* – with spiritual energy and impact; *"in the Holy Spirit"* for He knows the Saviour best, He knows the sinner best, He knows and speaks the message best. Only through Him is it *"in much assurance."* Only by His help do we have preaching with knowledge and conviction, and response that shows conviction and assurance. We must retain the grandeur of the message and never dilute it - for misrepresenting God is a disservice to Him and to the sinner.

This can be done quite easily, and perhaps with a desire to simplify the message, but it's a road that is fraught with danger. In an effort to make the message acceptable, some stray from being scriptural. For instance, some teach it is possible to fall away and be lost after salvation; others suggest that new converts can accept Jesus as Saviour, and, at a later stage, make Him Lord; and it has become popular for many to attempt leading souls to Christ by means of what is known as 'The sinner's prayer.' These beliefs and practices are biblically and evangelically unsound, and they conflict with the ministry of the Holy Spirit whose work it is to guide into all truth through conviction of sin and genuine repentance.

For faith to have substance, we need to present a message with substance. Even adherents of eastern religions can detect lack of substance in an 'easy-believism' gospel. This was the testimony of a Hindu man in South India who, after hearing weak presentations of the gospel, had never heard there's a glory to it, and concluded it was 'too simple.' No one ever told him about the glories of the Christ, yet they were trying to share the gospel. Scriptures like Acts 17:2-4 shows that the wealth of God's provision in sound gospel content lay at the foundation of the work in Thessalonica. It was the serious matter of reasoning ... explaining ... demonstrating ... and persuading. They didn't share it with a kind of eye-dropper approach, they immersed people in the gospel. Ignorant people whose lives were immersed in idolatry were treated to the glorious gospel of the happy God, because the preachers wanted His happiness to become theirs.

These are the four strong tracks of the gospel, which can never be replaced by anything less. The essentials of the gospel were at the core of the message. This was a carefully reasoned message that allowed something from the heart of his God to move Paul's heart and reach the heart of the sinner. Other portions, such as his letter to the Romans, include reasoning on regeneration, redemption, justification, glorification, and much more, so while the gospel may be simple in one way, it's never simplistic. As far as Paul was concerned, even crucifixion was a doctrine, and not only an action. Only two verses before speaking to Galatians about a crucified Christ being clearly portrayed or placarded before them[22], he said, *"I have been crucified with Christ."*

Such was his expectation that the truths of the gospel would become living realities to those who believe. His mission was placarding Christ, not placating people! Having been won to Christ, he wanted others also to say, *"I have been crucified with Christ; it is no longer I who live, but Christ lives in me, and the life which I now live in the flesh I live by faith in the Son of God who loved me and gave Himself for me."*[23]

"If any man speak" (1 Pet.4:11, KJV). Oh, we know that preaching is not always done publicly; sometimes, it's personal witness by one to another, but the same truths apply, and the same principles apply. The message whose content is carefully presented in public preaching should be identical to what is considered in private conversation. Challenging sinners and confronting sin are central to the gospel, and unless we challenge sin we cannot help sinners to find the Saviour. Like Paul, we have the opportunity to confront man's ungodliness by presenting Christ, *"the mystery of godliness."*[24] We know – don't we? – there can be no knowledge of salvation without knowing they are lost; no possibility of forgiveness without conviction, no rescue without repentance; no possibility of peace without being troubled, no pardon without guilt; no following the Saviour without forsaking sin; and no certainty of heaven without being faced with hell.

Sensitively, we can fulfil the kind of uncompromising preaching of which it was said that the preacher "shook people over hell." That's not insensitivity, is it? It's the burden of a man's heart that makes him sit with someone to face the unthinkable, so that friends we know should never fail to hear about hell because we didn't love them enough to tell them. It may be someone in our family, a relative; it may be a friend, someone in your neighbourhood or at work - can we not love them enough to speak to them about the Saviour? If it means warning them about hell, let us do it in the love of Christ.

We sometimes have opportunities in various settings to speak to men and women about their souls. Whether it's in public preaching or in private conversation, our aims are twofold: to make them feel comfortable in whatever setting it is, but that they will never feel comfortable with God until He makes them feel uncomfortable. We also want them to feel accepted wherever we meet them, but that they will never know acceptance with God until they know they are unacceptable without Christ as their Saviour. We are presenting a Person, not selling a product, therefore inviting lives that are ruined by ambition or addiction to "Try Jesus" is another gospel. Jesus Christ is for trusting, not trying. When we speak to them about their need, it's to bring them away from the mentality of trying. Their days of trying are over. It's now the decisive moment of trust.

He is not on trial, and we must emphasise the essentials and not be content with cosy homilies and anecdotal chats. Sinners come in their emptiness, nothingness, and hopelessness to discover that the cross is their only hope for eternity. The message is held out to each one, and it's the word of the message that will cause them to turn from darkness to light, and from the power of Satan to God. We won't see it happen, but at that moment they will be delivered from the power of darkness and conveyed into the kingdom of the Son of His love.[25]

The Kind of Preacher – the Character of the Messenger

Paul knew how essential it was that his message was true *"for the gospel's sake,"*[26] but it also was vital that the Thessalonians knew *"What kind of men"* had preached to them *"for your sake."* [17] They knew what kind of message was preached, and they also knew the kind of messengers who preached it. They had heard men preach an appealing message, *"as though God were pleading through"* them,[27] and gospel preachers can do no more. Sadly, they can do a lot less, for not all realise that the currency of the gospel has been stamped on two sides of the one coin: and they remain, *"for the gospel's sake"* and *"for your sake."* It takes both for the heart of God to plead through the heart of His preacher, and for His glory in the message to be complemented by His glory in the messenger. It's important that we know the kind of messengers God sends. They are:

Approved

This is divine approval in their God-given acceptability. It shows what God thinks of them, but this will lead to a discerned acceptability among their hearers. The Lord Jesus Christ showed that God the Father had set His seal on Him[28]: a seal of affection, approval and authority, and His messengers must reflect something of this too.

Entrusted

This is divine trust in their God-given fidelity. This shows what God does through them in their faithfulness to His Name and Word, and because He sees them as trustworthy. They are like the woman's broken flask of spikenard – Gr. *pistikos* – it was genuine, and its fragrance filled the home. This is what the gospel preachers should do: they bring the fragrance of Christ with the faithful Word, and they do it through brokenness. One aspect of this applies to what we could call 'priestly preaching.' 1 Peter 2:9 (RV) calls for those who know Christ as Priest to show *"forth the excellencies of Him who called you out of darkness into his marvellous light"* – not only the marvellous light of knowing the Saviour of the sinner, but the Lord of the follower.

As ambassadors of Christ, our commission is to bring others to know Him, so that they can discover Him as their Priest too. Does this give us the liberty to share our royal priesthood witness with other believers? If so, they would have similar freedom to share in the holy priesthood's worship in verse 5, but, since verse 5 doesn't permit an open table, verse 9 doesn't condone an open platform.

Tested

This is divine pleasure in their God-given authority. He sees them as twice tested, before Him and others, and this is good for there's nothing more powerful in the hands of God than a consistent messenger with a consistent message. Paul and Silas are great examples for any preacher. They were free *"from error"* – there was no deception or fallacy; they were free from *"uncleanness"* – there was no hidden immorality; and they were free from guile –

there was no slick trickery or gimmickry that they used as some sort of bait to entertain or entrap.

Jesus has commanded, *"Go therefore and make disciples of all the nations, baptising them"* into (RV) *"the name of the Father and of the Son and of the Holy Spirit, teaching them to observe all things that I have commanded you; and lo, I am with you always, even to the end of the age."*[29] This is His mandate. When we preach, we own it as our mandate, and when sinners respond, it should become their mandate. It's the baton of divine transferral. It's being serious about the great commission: emphasising the call to obedience to those who hear the gospel, so that they will see that believing is an act of obedience. When He said, *"I have given them Your word,"* what did He mean?

Was He referring to the Old Testament, from Genesis to Malachi, or was He not rather speaking about the revelation of His will that should energise their service with a transforming message? He was giving marching orders to witnesses of a gospel that demands obligation as well as reconciliation, and calling us to take His commission seriously by emphasising obedience in our preaching. The kind of gospel we preach will determine the kind of disciples we make! We must never become incomplete messengers with an incomplete message. That's not in our contract. Diluting the message always leads to diminishing the Saviour and deceiving the sinner.

Our highest aim in preaching is that it satisfies divine pleasure, and this means we should know what God feels about our kind of preaching and what it does to His heart. His pleasure in the gospel is at stake. Another danger lies in encouraging the unsaved to worship before they have yielded to Christ's ownership and discipleship. We must never invite unsaved sinners to do what God hasn't asked or fitted them to do. The preacher's greatest honour is to bring sinners to the blood of Jesus: to its shedding; and to its sprinkling.

SHEDDING

- Cleansing the sinner;
- Acceptance;
- Atonement;
- Union;
- Redemption.

SPRINKLING

- Claiming the saint;
- Obedience;
- Government;
- Communion;
- Obligation.

What a calling! Every blood-bought sinner is *"elect according to the foreknowledge of God the Father, in sanctification of the Spirit, for obedience and sprinkling of the blood of Jesus Christ."*[30] God's desire is that the knowledge of the preacher becomes the knowledge of the newly saved sinner, that the preacher's conviction will become their conviction, for this great reason, that they might be able to anticipate the *"for"* of their election.

Matthew and Mark both share the same telling message about the

Lord in Gethsemane – *"He went a little farther"*[31] – but there's a valuable difference. To Matthew, He is the King; to Mark, He is the Servant. It was just *"a little farther,"* humanly speaking for the lowly Servant, but a whole lot farther for the King of kings. Mark begins his gospel record by telling us that Jesus went *"a little farther"*[32] to call James and John and, near its end, of how He went *"a little farther"* to call on God. Perhaps it's time for His messengers to go a little farther, too, so that we will be closer to men, and closer to God.

In Acts 2:41 and 42, receiving the gospel was the first of seven spiritual experiences. If we lose the value of that number one lamp on the lampstand of divine testimony, it will be like removing one of the seven pillars of wisdom's house.[33] It will be like an army that has lost its sense of recruitment, like a school that has lost the need for enrolment, so also churches need to win souls - otherwise they will cease to exist.

In days when Christ is blasphemed and His Name taken in vain, when it's politically correct to ridicule Christianity, our world needs to hear a gospel that exalts the Saviour and excites the sinner, but they won't hear it without messengers who will explain the message. Do we know Him well enough or is there too much spiritual poverty? Are our hearts full enough or are we too often empty? Are our lives pure enough or are they affected by impurity?

In darkening days, our world needs to hear a brighter gospel, and the anticipation of the Saviour's return urges us to be among those who give it its proper place. We should preach as we have never preached before, reach as we have never reached before, and shine as we have never shone before. If we do, many will get a glimpse of His glory through the preaching and the preacher before the church goes home at the Rapture and the light of the world goes out. In one way, we have to take the message down to the people, but our highest honour is in bringing the people up to the message! Let's lift them up *"in power, in the Holy Spirit, and in much assurance"*[17] to see new horizons in the faith of the gospel, in the truth of the gospel, and in the hope of the gospel.[34]

Each new height reveals another
Far outshining every other,
And farther realms to conquer when it's gained.
On to higher peaks and pleasant,
Not content with just the present,
Ever upward and to heights not yet attained.
(Marjorie Lewis-Lloyd)

THE GLORIOUS GOSPEL

Its fundamental doctrines gleam afar;
Eternal in the heavens is their source;
Each penetrates our darkness like the star
That sets the boatman's sextant and his course.

Its monumental witness towers above
All earthly concepts, helping us to find
Deep thoughts of God, and evidence of love,
In nobler thoughts shaped in His noblest mind.

Invisible, yet by His works made known,
This all-creating God is clearly seen;
His hidden things are manifestly shown,
Revealed in time His everlasting plan.

Our non-judgemental God has made us free
From sin's dark presence, penalty and pow'r.
And now electing grace calls us to be
Conformed to His Son's image hour by hour.

Since death has lost its lordship over Him,
And having died to death He dies no more;
So, under grace, we live as dead to sin:
Its lordship gone from those whose sins He bore.
(A. McIlree)

3. CONTENTION: ON THE BASIS OF 'HOW?'

"... contend earnestly for the faith which was once for all delivered to the saints" (Jude v.3).

* * *

No competitor in a race would ever be allowed to begin one-eighth of the overall distance ahead of the starting line, and neither should any expositor. We would hardly imagine an Olympics' swimmer entering the pool over six metres ahead of other participants, yet it's not uncommon for some teachers to dive into Jude's twenty-five verses at verse three. Jude had no such intention. It was important to him that he assured his readers of what they are in Christ – called, beloved ... and preserved – to remind them that they are His by election, affection, and preservation. This would give them comfort in knowing that their temporal experience was permitted as part of their infinitely greater and eternal experience.

Paul gave an expanded version of this when he wrote so reassuringly to the church in Corinth:

> *"And since we have the same spirit of faith, according to what is written, 'I believed and therefore I spoke,' we also believe and therefore speak, knowing that He who raised up the Lord Jesus will also raise us up with Jesus, and will present us with you. For all things are for your sakes, that grace, having spread through the many, may cause thanksgiving to abound to the glory of God. Therefore we do not lose heart. Even though our outward man is perishing, yet the inward man is being renewed day by day. For our light affliction, which is but for a moment, is working for us a far more exceeding and eternal weight of glory, while we do not look at the things which are seen, but at the things which are not seen. For the things which are seen are temporary, but the things which are not seen are eternal."*[1]

Having provided comfort by reminding them of what they *are* in Christ, Jude immediately added encouragement by speaking of what they *have* in Christ – *"Mercy, peace, and love be multiplied to you."* How graciously he set the scene, that what they needed through Christ was based on what they were and what they had in Him. In other words, he wanted them to know that contending flows from mercy, peace, and love being demonstrated through those who are called, beloved, and preserved. They needed to be emboldened by the same "spirit of faith" that drew its well-founded confidence from all that is written about the faithfulness of God and of His promises in the gospel of Christ.

Contend Earnestly for the Faith

On the basis of this loving introduction, Jude came straight to the point and shared what the Spirit of God had shared with him: *"I found it necessary to write to you."* How good it is when we truly are in touch with Him and able to say, *"It seemed good to the Holy Spirit, and to us,"*[2] knowing that we are equally able to say, *"It seemed good to us, being assembled with one accord."*[3] Like these leaders, Jude sensed a need and, as his word for necessity implies, felt distressed by it (see the use of the same word in 1 Corinthians 7:26 and 1 Thessalonians 3:7). Having already called them *"beloved,"* he not only felt for them in their need but also was able to address it by *"the love of the Spirit."*[4] But what was this Spirit-led necessity? It pinpointed that he must urge them to sense the urgency of contending earnestly for the faith. Alerting them to the battleground of the faith is captured in the word *epagōnizesthai*, from which we get the thought of an agonising struggle.

His way of doing this was typically big-hearted. By *"exhorting"* (Gr. *parakaleō*: to call near or from beside) them, He wanted them to feel that he was close to the action, that his exhortation wasn't a shout from a distance, but meant he was close to them and calling alongside to comfort and entreat. He was well aware of what was going on among them and his approach was consistent with what Paul wrote to Philemon: *"Therefore, though I might be very bold in Christ to command you what is fitting, yet for love's sake I rather appeal* [Gr. *parakaleō] to you."*[5] In the same way, Jude appealed that his brethren should fight for what they believed, and it may be that he wondered if they had any fight left in them.

Had their spiritual energy been sapped by lengthy debate and argument? Had widening division weakened them? Or had they even been compromised by the manipulating influence of deepening friendships? It may be that fear kept them from countering heresy with truth. Being afraid of 'rocking the boat,' 'making matters worse,' or 'causing more trouble' could have seemed like good reasoning. They may even have become convinced that contending earnestly could be divisive; they could gain the core and lose the fringe. We have no way of knowing, but we do know that prolonged spiritual struggles deplete spiritual strength. False teachers know how to box clever, and those who defend the faith can be outwitted, out-thought and out-fought. All the more reason, then, that we show a willingness to fight for what we believe by learning how to *"fight the good fight of the faith"*;[6] not militantly, but biblically.

In 1965, two heavyweight boxers stepped into the ring in Lewiston, Maine, USA. Within two minutes of the first round, one was knocked down and promptly knocked out. He had been a contender, but not for long, and very quickly there was no fight left in him. Jude may have been concerned that his brethren had no fight left in them and were no longer real contenders. As Paul weathered his difficulties, he was able to say, *"We are hard-pressed on every side, yet not crushed; we are perplexed, but not in despair; persecuted, but not forsaken; struck down, but not destroyed."*[7] Some have rephrased the last clause and applied it in boxing terms as "knocked down, but not knocked out."[8]

Half-hearted conviction never leads to wholehearted commitment, and losing ground never leads to gaining the victory. They would never gain ground against false teachers if they didn't believe, love and practice the truth of God. The way forward would be a battle in which they must be actively engaged in the struggle to defend *"the faith,"* which would involve being faithful to it and with it. This implies a serious contest, but not one of being contentious! Jude obviously meant everyone to take this on board, and that no one should opt out and leave it to others to do the thinking. Every believer has a responsibility to learn, love and live the doctrines of the Lord, which He Himself said we should teach and that, in doing so, He would be with us to the end of the age.[9]

Of course, some say that 2016 marked the birth of the post-truth era, and this has been defined as "Relating to or denoting circumstances in which objective facts are less influential in shaping public opinion than appeals to emotion and personal belief."[10] Nothing could be farther from the truth, and we need to go back to before The Fall in the Garden of Eden to find a pre-lie period. It was the spawning ground of questioning, *"Has God indeed said?"*, and the place where falsifying His word began. The truth of God is clear-cut and, as believers, we must never give the impression that our beliefs are hazy and woolly or as unsubstantial as what some know as cotton candy or candy floss.

Jude's audience battled with their version of post-truth, centuries later so do we, and we need to ask if our understanding of what we believe matches:

- all things - Matthew 28:20;
- the way - Acts 18:26;
- the whole counsel of God - Acts 20:27;
- the faith - Romans 1:5;

- the truth -Galatians 5:7.

They will, if we:

- observe all things (Gr. *tērein* – from the same word used in Jude v.1 and v.21): By guarding and keeping our eye on what the Lord has commanded;
- explain the way (Gr. *exethento* – set out and expound);
- declare the whole counsel of God (Gr. *anangeilai* – to announce or tell as a messenger);
- obey the faith (Gr. *hupakoēn* – listening attentively);
- obey the truth (Gr. *peithesthai* – trust, agree, have confidence).

Each generation, including our own, must re-establish and re-emphasise doctrinal truth. Unsound teachers must meet more than their match with *"sound doctrine"*[11] and *"sound words"*[12] presented by those who are *"sound in the faith."*[13] Each overseer should give a lead in this by *"holding fast the faithful word as he has been taught, that he may be able, by sound doctrine, both to exhort and convict those who contradict."*[14] Following his example, there comes a point when men and women of God should become intolerant of tolerance. As already mentioned in chapter 1, this means we seek peace with honour, not peace at all costs; and unity that doesn't tolerate the adversity that comes from those who treat uniters as dividers.

It's right that those who love the Lord should love what He loves. Do we hold and emphasise what God holds and emphasises? Do we share what He has shared? It's essential that we do this for polarised opinions cannot possibly speak for Him or be given by

His Spirit. Very careful attention needs to be given whenever conflicting interpretations are made about anything in Scripture. The simple challenge is, are we being faithful to all that *"the faith"*[15] embraces?

Once for All Delivered

As we have already thought, God has given unchanging truth in the unchanging gospel of the unchanging Christ, and He has done it for all time, so we have every reason to trust the God who delivers. The real meaning is that He has surrendered it to us, that we in turn might be surrendered to Him.

- Once for all delivered (Jude 3) - **IT TO US;**
- To which you were delivered (Rom.6:17) - **US TO IT;**
- Who was delivered up (Rom.4:25) - **HIM TO US;**
- We are always delivered (2 Cor.4:11) - **US TO HIM.**

We have no idea how Jude's hearers responded, or how successful they were in healing believers who were damaged or in seeing false teachers won through the gospel. All we know is that his short letter was God's answer to the challenge. This was His remedy that should encourage the faithful, restore the fallen, and be able to convict the false. He could do no more than reflect the present-continuous implications in what Paul wrote to the church in Thessalonica: Keep on standing fast and keep on holding *"the traditions* [ordinances] *which you were taught, whether by word or our epistle."*[16]

A GORGEOUS ROBE

"Then Herod, with his men of war, treated Him with contempt and mocked Him,
arrayed Him in a gorgeous robe,[1] and sent Him back to Pilate"
[Gr. *lampros*: bright, clear, shining] (Lk.23:11)
"And they clothed Him with purple" (Mk.15:17)

Again and again, in constant, cruel jeering
These puny armies voiced their feeble scorn
Against the Man who knew His hour was nearing,
And taunted Him with royal robes and thorn.

For Jews, their kingly robe was bright and gorgeous:
A radiant garment made by men for men,
But while it shone, its glory was less glorious
Than heaven's Best who stood before them then.

The Gentile rulers saw this feeble effort
And tried to outperform what Jews had done.
Their purple robe was not designed for comfort,
But to demean the glories of God's Son.

Yet, none can divest Him of His own glory,
Nor can they invest any of their own;
This Kingly Man did this Himself more ably
By rising from His cross to fill the throne.

His rightful robe is clear, as clear[1] as crystal; (Rev.22:1)
His righteous clothing, whiter[1] than the light; (Rev.19:8)
The Root, the Branch, the offspring of King David, (Rev.22:16)
Heaven's great I AM eternally is Bright[1].

No *"gorgeous robe"* or *"purple"* can be fitting
Apparel for the glorious heavenly King;
The Saviour in Himself is the right clothing
And to Him Jew and Gentile need to cling.
(A. McIlree)

4. CONDEMNATION: ON THE BASIS OF 'WHAT?'

"For certain men have crept in unnoticed, who long ago were marked out for this condemnation, ungodly men, who turn the grace of our God into lewdness and deny the only Lord God and our Lord Jesus Christ. But these speak evil of whatever they do not know; and whatever they know naturally, like brute beasts, in these things they corrupt themselves. Woe to them! For they have gone in the way of Cain, have run greedily in the error of Balaam for profit, and perished in the rebellion of Korah. These are spots in your love feasts, while they feast with you without fear, serving only themselves. They are clouds without water, carried about by the winds; late autumn trees without fruit, twice dead, pulled up by the roots; raging waves of the sea, foaming up their own shame; wandering stars for whom is reserved the blackness of darkness forever" (Jude vv.4, 10-13).

* * *

Jude's salutation was all it took for a dividing line to be carved through the gathering, yet all he did was address the believers and no one else. Salvation always does this, of course; it confirms believers in their faith and in their security of being *"in Christ."* At the same time, it sets a spiritual division between believers and unbelievers, saved and lost, alive and dead, between light and darkness, the hopeful and the hopeless, between those who have been brought near to Christ and those who are far off, and between those who are true and those who are false.

When you love the Lord, and are loved by Him, the joy of being on the right side of these differences is very meaningful, yet many on the wrong side of the line find them completely meaningless. Before we go any farther, perhaps all of us should stop, either to feel the comfort of the following Scriptures as we read them or to sense their challenge if you have never known what it is to accept Christ as your Saviour.

- **In Christ** - *"There is therefore now no condemnation to those who are in Christ Jesus"* (Rom.8:1; 16:7);
- **Believers and unbelievers** - *"He who believes in Him is not condemned, but he who does not believe is condemned already, because he has not believed on the only begotten Son of God"* (Jn 3:18)
- **Saved and lost** - *"For the Son of Man has come to save that which was lost"* (Matt.18:11);
- **Alive or dead** - *"And you He made alive, who were dead in trespasses and sins"* (Eph.2:1);
- **In light or in darkness** - *"You were once darkness, but now you are light in the Lord"* (Eph.5:8);
- **Hopeful or hopeless** - *"Christ in you, the hope of glory"*

(Col.1:27). *"Having no hope and without God"* (Eph.2:12);
- **Near or far off**– *"But now in Christ Jesus you who once were far off have been brought near by the blood of Christ"* (Eph.2:13).

Creepers, Condemned and Corrupt

The problem among Jude's readers was real. In fact, it was very threatening. Being well aware of this, like any shepherd who wants to protect his flock, he faced up to the predators. When he referred to them as *"certain men,"* he really was saying, "these kind of men" for he knew what they were. His approach is enlightening, to say the least, for, instead of addressing them directly, he kept speaking to the church. Everything he had said so far was to believers about believers, but now he speaks, not to, but about the false teachers. This was sound principle and good practice for, although these men had wormed their way into the gathering, they didn't belong to that church. Those who don't belong to Christ don't belong among Christians, and those who don't belong to the church, which is His body, can't possibly belong to the local assembly.

For this reason, Jude immediately sets up one of his defining tripods and exposes these men as creepers, condemned, and corrupt. They were creepers, because they *"crept in unnoticed."* Their craftiness is captured in the Greek word *pareisdunō*, which is three words put together: *para* means beside, *eis* means into, and *duno* means go down; so, like foxes stalking sheep, they crept down in beside those of the little flock. They crept in unnoticed, but didn't stay unnoticed for long! They came in intentionally, but were not intentionally let in. Their disguise was so good, and their deportment so sly and convincing, that they had deceived the shepherds and come in by stealth.

Sadly, this wasn't the only place that suffered from this kind of infiltration. In 2 Corinthians 11:13-15, Paul warned the church about *"false apostles"* who were deceitful workers and cunning enough to transform themselves into ministers of righteousness. As he thought of the hazards he had faced, he lists *"perils among false brethren"* with what he had suffered by imprisonment and flogging, shipwreck, robbers, dangers among Jews and Gentiles, and battling high seas.[1] If anyone knew how dangerous these men were, Paul did, and they were part of his *"deep concern for all the churches."* He had seen through their disguise and concluded that their end will be according to their works.

Jude was of the same mind and was clear that they *"long ago were marked out for this condemnation."* God always sees and knows what's in the heart and mind of everyone,[2] and nothing goes unnoticed by Him. When the Lord Jesus Christ was on His way to Calvary He faced *"certain"* – the kind of men – *"who bore false witness against Him."*[3] He was on His way to die for the ungodly,[4] yet Peter speaks in his second letter about *"the day of judgement and perdition of ungodly men."*[5] God has marked them out – He has written beforehand – that their day of reckoning is coming.

Sheep Among Wolves

In the meantime, the Good Shepherd says, *"I send you out as sheep in the midst of wolves."*[6] His commission sets His sheep at the centre of hostility, just as He was. Psalm 22 describes Him as being surrounded by bulls, lions, dogs, and wild oxen; and how they attacked, and roared, and snarled, and gored! Psalm 118:12 adds, *"they surrounded Him like bees"* with stinging words and insults, and so He promised His own, *"If they persecuted Me, they will also persecute you."*[7] But the Lord didn't only say what they would face, He told His disciples how to face them. In His own ministry, He never retaliated, not even *"When they hurled their insults at Him,"*[8] so He told them to *"be wise as serpents and harmless as doves."*[8]

This would guide what they said, and how they said it, which takes wisdom for reasoning and warmth for appealing. It takes both. This is the Christian's best defence. Being wise means we know the Word and what it means; being harmless means we know how to share it in the gentleness and love of our Saviour who was depicted by the turtledove in the burnt offering,[9] and by the bridegroom of the Song of Songs whose eyes were like doves.[10] However, we will be poorly equipped if we try to have one without the other. On its own, clear reasoning isn't enough; neither is warm appealing.

There are wolves who want to tear our reasoning to shreds, and some know the Bible well enough to mount their thought-out arguments, so we need to know God's Word better than they do. It's paramount, but we also need to know how to use it. Left to ourselves, we would be like Peter with his brandished sword in Gethsemane. In the place where the heart of the Saviour was moved so deeply, His disciple was ready to show that his mind wasn't harmless. We need the mind of the Spirit, if we want to share the mind of Christ. There's never any shortage of great debates, but we are not out to win the argument, we want to win the arguer!

Wolves Among Sheep

There's a big difference between sheep being in the middle of wolves and wolves being in the middle of sheep. The first is where we are meant to be, and the second is where they are not meant to be. In the first, we go to them; in the second, they "come to you."[11] The intentions are not mutual. The sheep want to see wolves changed by being drawn to life in Christ; the wolves want to see His sheep drawn away from Him and their love for Him killed off. The problem is that these wolves don't come among the flock looking like wolves; they come looking like sheep and looking for sheep. Around seven hundred years earlier, Zephaniah the prophet said that Jerusalem's judges were *"evening wolves that leave not a bone till morning."*[12] It was the same old story - they were wolves dressed as judges.

It was different in Nehemiah's day and, if anything, worse. It's bad when wolves come in unnoticed, but worse when they are invited in! With their captivity in Babylon over, the people were kept busy rebuilding the wall of Jerusalem, and even Eliashib the high priest was involved. By all appearances, he was living up to the meaning of his name, God will restore, as he built the Sheep Gate with its doors and wall and towers. What a force for good, yet tragedy was to come. The very man who built the Sheep Gate was the first to let in a wolf. Ironically, the man he welcomed was the one who taunted Nehemiah and the builders by saying, *"if even a fox goes up on it, he will break down their stone wall."*[13]

But, sadly, he didn't have to walk on it for he was allowed to walk through it. The wolf was allowed to enter the gate that was built as the entrance for sacrifices that were going to the altar, and, once inside, he was given a place of residence. Eliashib had become a close friend of Tobiah. Too close, in fact! The word used to describe their alliance is *qarowb*, a kinsman, as Boaz was to Naomi and Ruth,[14] but Eliashib and Tobiah were never kinsmen. To make a boarding place for the wolf, Eliashib emptied the storeroom that kept the meal offering, the frankincense, the tithes of grain, the new wine and oil, which were commanded to be given to the Levites and singers and gatekeepers, and the offerings for the priests.[15]

If ever two men failed to live up to the meaning of their names, they did. 'God will restore' and the 'goodness of Jehovah' should have been a merger that signified great things, but not at this price. This storeroom should have been a safe house for the service of God, in a safe passage from the doorkeepers at the gate to the priests at the altar. But the way was badly compromised, and this may have had its roots in a marriage between one of Eliashib's grandsons and a daughter of Sanballat. How sad it is when family relationships distort spiritual judgement!

With tears running down their faces, Paul left the elders from Ephesus on the beach at Miletus, and one of the sobering thoughts he left with them was that *"savage wolves will come in among you, not sparing the flock."*[16] He urged them to pay attention, to take care of themselves in their role as elders and of the flock God had given them. As part of this, from then on they would be on the lookout for wolves. How would they know them? The Lord Jesus said, *"You will know them by their fruits."*[17] They can be identified by what they are, what they do, and by what they have: by their nature, their tactics, and by what they produce. Paul says they are *"men of corrupt minds and destitute of the truth, who suppose that godliness is a means of gain. From such men withdraw yourself.*"[18]

A Threefold Denial

Jude's concern was that his brothers and sisters needed help to identify the character and conduct of the false teachers among them. He was in no doubt that the grace of God meant nothing to them, and that they wanted to influence those to whom it meant everything. These men were indecent and their corruption corrupted God's truth and grace. One thing we can be sure of is that grace never condones sin, it condemns it; it never excuses sin, it accuses it. Their underlying problem was that they had never died with Christ and therefore couldn't die to sin! Only dying with Him lets us die to it. Even in the present day, some gospel preaching makes little of sin and repentance and much of love and forgiveness; little of lordship and much of freedom, little of change and much of professing. It mistakes free grace for cheap grace and, in its own way, changes *"the truth of God into a lie."*[19]

These men made an outright denial of who the Saviour is, and kept on actively rejecting grace as the only means of salvation. They denied Him as *"the only Lord"* – *ton monon despotēn* – meaning they refused to have His sovereign and absolute rule. They denied Him as Lord – *kurios* – by refusing to acknowledge His divine authority; and they denied Him as the Christ, the anointed Messiah. True believers have no difficulty in saying that He is the Christ,[20] but these men rejected His Deity and authority, the Master and His mastery. Their continuing condition dictated their continuing action, so they had nothing in common with *"common salvation,"* and no fellowship with God and Christ.[21] It could never be said of them, *"you all are partakers with me of* grace,"[22] or that they were *"partakers of the divine nature, having escaped the corruption that is in the world through lust."*[23]

Cain, Balaam and Korah

This is another of Jude's tripods, and it presents three aspects of failure that motivated the false teachers. They were defilers, rejecters and blasphemers, and in this triplet (Jude 1:8) they were identified with:

- A challenge to worship in Cain;
- A challenge to stewardship in Balaam;
- A challenge to leadership in Korah.

Each of these is an example of showing opposition to the will of God. Cain had no reaction until God indicated that He had found pleasure in Abel's offering, but had not seen the same in his. We know from Hebrews 11:4 that Abel's faith in God supported his offering, whereas it was absent in Cain. These early days were no different from now, in that faith is founded on what God has said, and we can assume that both sons heard something through their parents. Hebrews makes it clear that Abel's faith was the basis of his offering, and also was the foundation of his righteousness and witness. In Cain's lack of faith, all three were missing. On a personal level, he was like the people of Israel when they failed to enter God's rest because *"the word which they heard did not profit them, not being mixed with faith in those who heard it."*[24] God had seen the blood of Abel's offering, but, instead of bloodshed in Cain's offering, the only bloodshed was in his sin of killing his brother.

The absence of faith spoke loudly in Cain, and the sound of his faithless voice was as displeasing to God as his offering. In contrast to Cain's living without faith, Abel died in faith, yet even then a voice was heard for God was able to say, *"The voice of your brother's blood cries out to Me from the ground."*[25] What a hard way it was for Cain to learn that *"Without faith it is impossible to please Him."*[26] If only faith had awakened its expectation of God and caused him to cry out, like David, *"Deliver me from the guilt of bloodshed, O God."*[27] This was very relevant to the false teachers Jude was thinking about, for it described their hostility toward the believers that Jude commended. Cain was the first wolf to kill one of God's sheep, and instead of being convicted by the acceptance of Abel's offering, he resented it and deprived his brother from ever offering another. Undoubtedly, these false men had the same intention.

Like Balaam, they had their eyes on personal gain, but they certainly didn't set a precedent. Judas Iscariot had his eye on the bag.[28] Long before him, there was Elisha's servant, Gehazi, who certainly knew how to run greedily after Naaman for wealth he would never spend and clothes he would never wear.[29] In Balaam's case, his hand was reaching out to the bribing hand that brought *"the diviner's fee,"*[30] and he *"loved the wages of unrighteousness* [wrong-doing, RV]*."*[31] He is a great example of the often misunderstood proverb, *"A man's gift makes room for him, and brings him before great men."*[32] God knew that the temptation would be there, and gave an early warning of it when He said, *"You shall take no bribe, for a bribe blinds the discerning and perverts the words of the righteous."*[33] It has ruined individuals, but there were times when it permeated God's people too.

Micah was particularly burdened about it, and wrote, *"Her heads judge for a bribe, her priests teach for pay, and her prophets divine for money. Yet they lean on the Lord, and say, 'Is not the Lord among us? No harm can come upon us.'"* And then he added, *"The prince asks for gifts, the judge seeks a bribe, and the great man utters his evil desire; so they scheme together."*[34] How well these earlier failures summed up the craving of the false teachers who *"ran greedily"* after profit! Jude's word for them was *ekcheo*, which means "poured out," so they didn't suffer from the slight temptation of a dripping desire, but from a gushing urge for gain.

Their third resemblance was to Korah whose challenge to Moses and Aaron in Numbers 16 showed defiance at its worst. In blatant confrontation, they accused their mediator and high priest of unwarranted dominance, and claimed that both holiness and the LORD were as much among the congregation as with each of them. After God's judgement had fallen on two hundred and fifty leaders, the agitation stirred the people to further complaint, and by the end of that day the death toll had risen to almost fifteen thousand. It was brought to an end when Aaron, for the first and only time that we know of, ran among the people with a censer containing fire from the altar and incense.

It was a graphic demonstration of the fire from the altar of God and the fragrance of Christ combined in the urgency of atonement.[35] If only the false teachers had listened, and learned that man's rebellion has only two outcomes: either they fall under the judgement of God or their plague is stopped by acceptance of the sacrifice of the Lord Jesus Christ and the merits of His atonement. The sequel to Korah's sin was that their two hundred and fifty copper censers were gathered up and hammered into thin plates as a covering for the altar. From then on, there was a reminder on the altar for every offerer that sin's **guilt** had been judged. The only other record of thin plates is in Exodus 39:3 where gold was beaten into plates and fine wires, and then interwoven with the tabernacle's colours. In a very distinct way, God arranged for the gold to be worked into each fibre: in the blue, in the purple, in the scarlet, and in the white fine linen. In this way He foreshadowed Christ's heavenliness, kingliness, lowliness, and righteousness, with **glory** at the heart of each.

These two precedents occurred on the same day: the high priest ran, and the memorial of judgement was fixed to the altar. It's a noticeable omission in the four gospel accounts that, when the Lord Jesus Christ was on earth, there is no indication that He ever ran. He stood, walked, sat, knelt and lay, but no mention of anything that caused Him to run. However, when His work on earth was over, the letter to the Hebrews describes His entrance to glory at the end of chapter 6 as the Forerunner. What a difference! He was entering into the presence of God as High Priest, and the end of chapter 2 depicts His ministry as being *"able to aid."* This time, instead of the word *prodromos* for the Forerunner, He is presented by the word *boēēthēsai*, which means to help or succour. It's interesting that it includes the Greek word *theō* and gives the thought that He runs to help those who call. How lovely to think that Aaron is recorded as having run only once, in judgement, yet Christ our great High Priest is constantly seen as running for our blessing.

All three examples of Cain, Balaam and Korah held a powerful condemnation for these false men for each of them stood for falsehood in one way or another. Cain's attempt to please God in worship was false; Balaam's attempt to prophesy was false, and the whole basis of Korah's attempt to gain priestly service was false. Worshippers, prophets and priests need to be genuine, and all falsehood means living a lie. This brought judgement from God in each case and a loud warning to false teachers that they were guaranteed to face it too.

Rocks, Clouds, and Trees

With this tripod, Jude had no intention of leaving the false teachers with no idea of what God thought of them. He didn't hold back in the slightest and, as we would say, he knew how to call a spade a spade! We could be tempted to say, tongue in cheek, "Hey Jude, could you come to the point? Can you make yourself clear?" But there's no need for such irony for the real speaker is the Spirit of God. His hard-hitting lessons came in pairs from sea, land and sky, and they should have been deeply convicted by what He said.

1. *They are rocks ... and raging waves*

The New King James Version speaks about *"spots,"* but this relates to the Greek word *spilos* – a spot or defect. The intended word *spilas* refers to a reef or hidden rocks in the sea. The thought of hidden rocks allows us immediately to think of unnoticed things, just as these men had been, but they are no longer unnoticed. God has His own way of bringing things to light, and even hidden rocks can be brought to the surface! Jude senses that it's time for suitably gifted men to speak up. He would have known that among the spiritual gifts given to the church (1 Cor.12:28) was the particular ministry of *"administrations"* or, in other translations, *"governments."*

Both of these words can be rather misleading when we think of how we normally understand and apply them. The word *kubernēsis* is related to the helmsman or pilot (*kubernētēs*) of a ship. This implies someone who knows the currents and the undercurrents, the shallows, rocks and reefs, and is able safely to steer the vessel. He knew it was a time for spiritual helmsmen to pilot his brothers and sisters through troubled waters, and there are still times when the same spiritual skills are needed. Good helmsmen prevent shipwreck, and are God's antidote to false teachers. Their spiritual perception will detect menacing signs of danger and guide God's people clear of the shipwrecking intentions of evil men.

One version of the Scriptures (RSV) translates *kubernēsis* as "administrators," and this ambiguous connotation doesn't give the right sense at all. Naturally, there will be times when the practicalities of church funds, and correspondence need an administrator, but this is not what the spiritual gift implies. Unsaved men and women can be qualified administrators, but only redeemed men and women can be endued with the spiritual gift of spiritual navigation. As raging waves in a troubled sea, false men stir up lots of mire and dirt, and prevent peace.[36] Wild billows churn up all sorts of filth. As many beaches testify, disgrace has the habit of resurfacing! To its shame, church history shows that churches can testify to it as well, but our Chief Helmsman gives this assurance to those who take His word: *"Do not fear them. For there is nothing covered that will not be revealed, and hidden that will not be known."*[37]

2. Shepherds ... autumn trees

Jude's readers were in a battleground where those who were

Christ-centred were under attack by those who were self-centred. To illustrate this, God says they were *"serving themselves,"* and His word for serving is the word *poimainō* – "shepherding." Instead of being God-appointed shepherds of the sheep, they were self-appointed shepherds of themselves. This was a fruitless exercise, for in their emptiness they were worse than the people of Israel whom the Lord portrayed as a barren fig tree. They had nothing but leaves, and these autumn trees were leafless as well as fruitless. And being rootless, they would remain so! In fact they were dead, pulled up by the roots and grounded in nothing, so they were twice dead: getting and giving nothing. Faith had never been sown in these ungodly men, so there could never be a harvest through faith. They were faithless and fruitless and must have looked so different from those who were planted in the house of the Lord! [38] It would make us wonder if leaders were emboldened to tell them so, by pointing out that Jude's letter had exposed them.

3. *Clouds ... wandering stars*

Solomon said, *"If the clouds are full of rain, they empty themselves upon the earth,"*[39] but these men were empty. They were all bulk and no water, and Solomon had this kind of individual in mind when he went on to say, *"Whoever falsely boasts of giving is like clouds and wind without rain."*[40] They were bone dry, and there was only one reason for this: they had never been refreshed in Christ and couldn't refresh others. They were wandering stars, the opposite of those that were set in their galaxies by the Lord and by which men can set their compass. Of these, God has said, *"Lift up your eyes on high, and see who has created these things, who brings out their host by number; He calls them all by name, by the greatness of His might and the strength of His power, not one is missing."*[41]

By contrast, meteors and comets that are nameless to God flash across the sky as its evidence of a fallen creation. What an apt description of false teachers who shoot off at tangents and go headlong into darkness!

With much thankfulness to God, we take our place among His servants who have heard His desire, *"that you may become blameless and harmless, children of God without fault in the midst of a crooked and perverse generation, among whom you shine as lights in the world."*[42] And we do this knowing that, *"Those who are wise shall shine like the brightness of the firmament, and those who turn many to righteousness like the stars forever and ever."*[42]

ALL YOUR WAVES
Psalms 42:7; 88:7

Like Him whose power was seen as much
In death, as in His infancy,
Waves in their birth, and in their death,
May never lose their potency;
Yet waves pre-set to sweep o'er Him,
And destined long before His birth,
Were formed while He was still in heaven,
Their deluge sent to crash on earth.

A course determined on the throne
By the eternal Trinity
Was fixed to end at Calvary's cross
On Christ 'mid man's brutality.
God's waves collided on Him there,
Each billow judgement-driven,
To bring us sinners to His cross
And to His throne in heaven.

As much as when in Galilee,
With waves and billow's bearing down,
He slept, unthreatened by the sea
That threatened those who were with Him;
Yet well He knew a greater storm
Would threaten Him, but not His own,
And give eternal rest to those
For whom He would for sin atone.

And now there is no storm to face,
The cross for Him, and us, is past.
The transient billows, by His grace,
Have given way to perfect peace.
Wave after wave, through precious blood,
Of peace secured, an endless flow,
Beginning in the heart of God
And ending in our hearts below.

His waves of wrath forever past,
His waves of peace forever last!
And what was birthed by Him above
Has birthed in us undying love.
(A. McIlree)

5. REVELATION: ON THE BASIS OF 'WHEN?'

Those who want to defeat their enemy must have victory with God. Jude certainly did, and his knowledge of how to handle false teachers flowed from his knowledge of God and His Word. Having charted their character with his tripods:

- Cain, Balaam and Korah;
- Rocks, clouds and self-serving shepherds;
- Waves, stars and trees.

... he made a devastating assessment of them, but wasn't finished. The careful servant of God always makes sure that his view is well-founded, and it soon becomes evident to present-day disciples of the Lord Jesus Christ that divine revelation is to Jude's tripod what a laser level is to a surveyor's. Jude knew, and still teaches his readers, that withstanding false teachers and dismantling false teaching is inseparably connected to knowing what God has revealed. Shallowness gives no defence, so refuge must be found in the security of biblical revelation and reasoning.

Jeremiah wrote about Dedan and of how they were advised to "*dwell deep,*"[1] which meant they should find refuge in a place that was far from the fringes where they would be exposed to invasion. In a military sense, they were to dig themselves in, which is a graphic illustration of what believers should do. Living on the fringe of scriptural understanding leaves us vulnerable to attack, but the more we *"dwell deep"* the better we will be at contending earnestly for the faith. With this in mind, Jude presented three examples of how God has dealt with hostile opposition.

Unbelieving Israelites, Angels, Sodom and Gomorrah

One of God's great principles is that *"righteousness exalts a nation, but sin is a reproach to any people."*[2] The contrast is so stark: righteousness "lifts up" and sin is "wicked."[3] Jude's examples span earth and heaven, time and eternity, redeemed and unregenerate, and show the affront that sin is to the holiness of God. They also show a consistent response from *"Him who judges righteously."*[4]

The People

The adversary delights in alluring individuals into sin, but also does all he can to disrupt God-centred gatherings. Who would have thought that His people would have been so badly affected in their wanderings between the Red Sea and the Jordan? Even though the great Redeemer took them out of Egypt, this didn't take Egypt out of them, and unbelief robbed them of going into the land of Canaan. God took care of the advancing Egyptian army as it attempted to overtake them in their escape, and promised, *"The Egyptians whom you see today, you shall see again no more forever."*[5] Nevertheless, others came shortly afterwards, and it's on record that Amalek attacked their rear ranks: *"all the stragglers at your rear."*[6]

Once again, God promised that the memory of Amalek would be blotted out from under heaven for what they had done, yet the people had a much bigger lesson to learn. Their greatest enemy wouldn't attack from behind, but from within; they would become their own worst enemy until the wilderness became a graveyard. The book of Numbers tells its own story: in fact, it could be called the book of dwindling numbers!

- In chapter 14 – The influence of ten spies who brought back a "bad report" from Canaan was seen in a mass outbreak of rebellion among the people, to the extent they defied and rejected God and wanted to stone Joshua and Caleb. This resulted in God slaying the ten and condemning the whole generation to death in the wilderness, with the promise that only Joshua and Caleb would survive;
- In chapter 16 – Two hundred and fifty men were killed for their part in Korah's rebellion, and fourteen thousand seven hundred died in the following plague;
- In chapter 21 – An unknown number died after being bitten by fiery serpents;
- In chapter 25 – Twenty-four thousand died in the plague that accompanied the sin at Baal Peor;
- In chapter 26:65 – God referred to His earlier promise in chapter 14:29 that a whole generation would die and, true to His Word, only Joshua and Caleb survived of all who had been counted in the earlier census.

By referring his readers to God's dealings with the people of Israel, Jude left them in no doubt that He remains faithful to His Word, whether in blessing or in judgement. He had described the people as murmurers and complainers, and these are the words Jude would use in verse 16 regarding the false teachers (RV). He had reminded them of Balaam who, in spite of himself, had to tell Balak, *"God is not a man, that He should lie, nor a son of man that He should repent. Has He said, and will He not do? Or has He spoken, and will He not make it good?"*[7] This is the point that the false teachers should have taken to heart as soon as Jude stated they were marked out for condemnation. In their state of denying the Lord, it was irreversible. They also should have recognised that God thwarted Balak's plans, and would do the same with theirs. Had He not said, and would He not do? Moses' prayer in Psalm 90 holds a sad summary of Israel's wilderness experience: *"We have been consumed by Your anger, and by Your wrath we are terrified ... For all our days have passed away in Your wrath."*[8]

Angels

The greatest God-centred gathering the adversary ever disrupted was in heaven. Before the physical creation of Genesis 1, God created His angelic host with perfectly ordered ranks and seniority, and character suited to the Triune presence. Their harmony of character and purpose was wonderfully demonstrated when, in unison, *"the morning stars sang together, and all the sons of God shouted for joy"*[9] when the foundations of the earth were laid. Such was their response to seeing its Creator, and theirs, at work.

His mention of an innumerable company[10] refers to the present gathering around His throne of angels that are *"of God ... holy ... His ... mighty ... and elect."*[11] It is of this gathering that we read, *"He makes His angels spirits, His ministers a flame of fire,"*[12] meaning they instantly fulfil His will, and speedily like wind and lightning. They also are said to be *"ministering spirits sent forth to minister for those who will inherit salvation."*[13] This speaks of them fulfilling a dual role in their service: *leitourgika*, toward God in heaven like temple worshippers; *diakonian*, toward believers on earth as helpers on their journey to the salvation that is ready to be revealed in the last time.[14]

Before all this earthward service began, an even greater host surrounded the LORD of hosts until Satan led a rebellion that led to his fall. The Lord Jesus Christ said, *"I saw Satan fall like lightning from heaven,"*[15] which conveys how quickly he was judged and removed, along with those who were banished with him. John gives a graphic account in Revelation 12:4 when he says that the dragon's *"tail drew a third of the stars of heaven,"* and this may indicate the size of following he generated. If so, it shows the forces on which he has been able to draw throughout his efforts to topple the purposes of God on earth.

Paul has left us in no doubt about their activity in the heavenly places and how their influence lies behind the human face of opposition believers experience. We may feel that we are wrestling with human hostility, but he makes it clear that we are up against greater forces than men, beginning with the devil himself. Then Paul adds, *"For we do not wrestle against flesh and blood, but against principalities, against powers, against the rulers of the darkness of this age, against spiritual hosts of wickedness."*[16] They once belonged to Jehovah of hosts, but now they are hosts of wickedness who had forfeited:

- The glory of heaven for everlasting chains;
- Eternal light for eternal darkness;
- God-given liberty for Satanic bondage.

Peter reasoned that *"if God did not spare the angels who sinned, but cast them down to hell and delivered them into chains of darkness, to be reserved for judgement,"*[17] then judgement also awaits false teachers. Jude's comment is similar – *"And the angels who did not keep their proper domain, but left their own abode, He has reserved in everlasting chains under darkness for the judgement of the great day."* In telling us they *"did not keep their proper domain"* (Gr. *archē*), Jude means they didn't hold fast to the principality (Gr. *archē*) God had given them; and they are now principalities under the direction of the devil.

How persuasive the devil must be! It was one thing for him to enter the Garden of Eden to deceive Eve, quite another to operate among the host of heaven and spread his lies there in the belief of having an effect. Why did the omniscient God not challenge him as soon as the thought came into his mind or as he whispered it among other angelic beings? The only reason we can assume is that the eternal purpose of the Father, Son and Holy Spirit to redeem had already been formed, and that the fall of Satan was permitted in the sure knowledge of Their sovereignty that it would lead to His purpose being fulfilled.

Sodom and Gomorrah

Well could we, again, apply the stark contrast of Proverbs 14:34, but this time it is seen in looking at 'before and after' descriptions. When Lot looked at the landscape before him, he saw *"that it was well watered everywhere* [before the Lord destroyed Sodom and Gomorrah] *like the garden of the LORD, like the land of Egypt as you go toward Zoar.*"[18] Twenty years later, according to Newberry, Abraham gazed on a very different scene when *"he looked toward Sodom and Gomorrah, and toward all the land of the plain; and he saw, and behold, the smoke of the land which went up like the smoke of a furnace."*[19] Sadder still, it never recovered. More than four centuries later, when God was about to speak to Moses about his death, He mentioned it again: *"The whole land is brimstone, salt, and burning; it is not sown, nor does it bear, nor does any grass grow there, like the overthrow of Sodom and Gomorrah, Admah, and Zeboim, which the Lord overthrew in His anger and His wrath."*[20] How could anyone want these in exchange for the lush conditions they had known? Barrenness and dryness instead of being well watered; and how could anyone want to lose the beauty and fertility that was like the garden of the LORD?

God's people had forfeited all the blessings associated with entering the land and His rest, a place they would never see,[21] angels forfeited their place around the throne of God and the holy atmosphere of His presence, the place and the Person they would never see again; and Sodom and Gomorrah lost conditions they would never reclaim. The people of Israel went after things that were false and ungodly; angels believed a lie from the father of lies[22] and turned from their only Master and Lord; and Sodom and Gomorrah went after the false pleasures of their filthy talk and walk.

Jude must have touched raw nerves as, by the leading of the Spirit of God, he highlighted the three areas of falsehood that the false teachers promoted among his readers, and as he fearlessly assured them of the impending wrath and judgement of God. Just as death, darkness and a day of reckoning, and fire were the lot of the people, angels, and Sodom and Gomorrah, so the false teachers were under the same condemnation. At the same time, the dear fellow-believers must have taken heart from all that applied to them:

- Like the people who fled from Egypt, they also had fled from bondage, having escaped the corruption that is in the world;[23]
- Like the angels who never fell, they were devoted to their only Master and Lord, Jesus Christ. Because of this, they also could rejoice in being *"of God ... holy ... His ... mighty ... and elect"*[24];
- Like Sodom and Gomorrah in their former state, they were cultivated as God's tilled land[25] with its accompanying features of order, beauty, fragrance and growth being the testimony of their lives both individually and as a gathered company of the Lord's people.

What They Knew

So there was much to condemn the false and commend the faithful. Jude knew that they knew what he was speaking about, though this isn't clear in some versions. In verse 5, the New King James Version says, "I want to remind you, though you once knew this," but other versions make it clearer:

- ASV – *"though ye know all things once for all"*;
- NASB – *"though you know all things once for all"*;
- RSV – *"though you were once for all fully informed"*;
- NRSV – *"though you are fully informed"*;

- RV – *"though ye know all things once for all."*

By reminding them, Jude brought matters to the forefront of their minds so that they were more fully prepared *"to contend earnestly for the faith which was once for all delivered to the saints"* (RV) – and the point is, including to them!

What They Never Knew

Up until now, Jude has been reminding believers of what is recorded in the Old Testament Scriptures, but now there's a change. He moves from former revelation to fresh revelation by current inspiration, just as Paul did when he named Jannes and Jambres[26] as the magicians who opposed Moses in Exodus 7 and 8. Jude's new information must have carried enormous weight with the company of believers. Suddenly, they must have realised that Jude was sharing things that had never been heard before, and in this privilege they must have been greatly encouraged to handle their opposition.

Michael the Archangel

Jude's first disclosure enlightened them to the dispute that took place between Michael the Archangel and the devil about the burial of Moses' body. There is no mention of this in Deuteronomy 34, and its emphatic comment is, that *"He [God] buried him … but no one knows his grave to this day."* God chose the resting place for the body of His servant and friend,[27] and the devil doesn't know the place. Had the devil buried him, God would have known the place, so even on this point Jude was stating that God is sovereign, and the devil isn't. Had the people known, he could have misled them into misplaced hero worship, venerating the man, and promoting pilgrimage to his grave. Jebel Musa, the mountain of Moses, is an example of this. Visitors can climb its 3,700 steps of repentance that were cut out by a monk, and on their ascent they can visit a monastery, a mosque, a chapel to Mary, the Spring of Elijah and the cave where the Lord is said to have visited him. Religious men love monuments and shrines, and the adversary has used them well to distract countless men and women from God and from true worship, not least in the case of Mary.

As Michael contended with the devil, he made no attempt to bring *"a reviling accusation"* against him. He had been there when Satan led his rebellion in heaven. He watched as he and his rebel angels were cast out of heaven. He had seen the supremacy of God and the sentence He passed on His adversary, but he made no reference to any of this. Nor did he make any judgemental remark on the devil's inability to know what God knows. Instead, he simply said, *"The Lord rebuke you!"*

What a lesson for these believers and for us! In the power of the cross, we have been delivered from one who is too strong for us,[28] and should be careful what we say about him. He and his angels are a mighty force, and well may we say, *"We have no power against this great multitude that is coming against us; nor do we know what to do, but our eyes are upon You."*[29] Protected by the whole armour of God and righteousness, we stand against the devil's methods, and with it we can *"withstand"* evil and *"resist"* him.[30] Both words are identical – *anthistēmi* – meaning we oppose him in the righteous character of our Lord Jesus Christ, but leave it to God to rebuke him. On this side of Calvary's triumph over the devil and his works,[31] we can trust Him to say it for us: *"The LORD rebuke you, Satan!"*[32]

What a lesson for false men, too! The One whom they denied is the One who censured the devil, and the debate ended with the potency of His word. How could they hear what Jude was disclosing about the devil's tactics and not take on board the implications for themselves? Jude knew the reason. While he knew there were things the assembly knew and didn't know, he also was aware what kind of men these were.

Brute Beasts

Sometimes, ignorance has a loud voice. Jude's description wasn't complimentary, but he knew how irrational and ferocious these men were. Put literally, his words could be translated as 'unreasonable animals,' and they were mixing with men and women of God who were threatened by their perverted and predatory ways. In verse 8, he says they are defilers, despisers and blasphemers who, as dreamers, live in the unreality of their false profession and teaching. They:

- defile the flesh - living in the filthiness of the flesh;
- reject authority - disregarding and despising Lordship, honour and worship;
- speak evil of - blaspheming and railing against authority, both earthly dignitaries and heavenly.

In contrast to the believers who knew what they knew and didn't know, these men blasphemed what they didn't know and their lives withered under the influence of what they did know. Natural knowledge darkened them in their darkness, yet spiritual knowledge never enlightened them for spiritual things are spiritually discerned and not received by the natural man.[33]

Enoch

In the same way that he received formerly undisclosed details from the Holy Spirit about Michael, Jude proceeds to share what he has been told about Enoch. Most of what we know of him is gleaned from the early chapters of Genesis. For instance, he walked with God for 300 years after the birth of his son, Methuselah, which may have marked a turning point in his life as a 65-year-old man.[34] During those three hundred years, he enjoyed communion with God and walked in step with His purpose, until the day came when it was as if he walked farther than ever. His Companion didn't change, but the scenery did as he left earth and was taken into eternity.

Peter describes Noah as a preacher of righteousness,[35] and now Jude indicates that Enoch was a preacher of judgement to come. The Genesis account of his life makes no mention of his prophetic ministry, yet Jude makes it clear that this was a vital part of his walk with God. The obvious truth is, of course, that if Enoch preached this message then he received it from God as he walked with Him, even though the timing of the event to which he referred was not made known to him. Even so, from his distant outpost of almost five and a half thousand years ago, he was specific about its purpose. He knew:

- **The Lord will come** – to reign on earth;
- **Who will come with Him** – with His saints;
- **Why He will come** – to judge the ungodly;

· **What He will judge** – ungodly deeds, ways, and speech.

The Lord Jesus Christ spoke about this in Matthew 13:41-43 when He said, *"The Son of Man will send out His angels, and they will gather out of His kingdom all things that offend, and those who practice lawlessness, and will cast them into the furnace of fire. There will be wailing and gnashing of teeth. Then the righteous will shine forth as the sun in the kingdom of their Father. He who has ears to hear, let him hear!"* It was later given to the apostle Paul to add that the time is coming, *"when the Lord Jesus is revealed from heaven with His mighty angels, in flaming fire taking vengeance on those who do not know God, and on those who do not obey the gospel of our Lord Jesus Christ. These shall be punished with everlasting destruction from the presence of the Lord and from the glory of His power, when He comes, in that Day, to be glorified in His saints and to be admired among all those who believe."*[36]

Ungodly

It's understandable that walking with God made Enoch very concerned about ungodliness, and the closer we are to God and his holiness the more we will be, too. He was concerned about ungodly people with their ungodly works done in ungodly ways, and the ungodly harshness of words spoken by ungodly sinners. Four times he emphasised the wicked and their wickedness, and Jude adds a fifth and sixth in verses 4 and 18 to describe the character and walk of these false men.

He knew all about their works and ways and words and walk, exposing them as evil speakers, grumblers, complainers, flatterers and mockers.[37] They were master fault-finders, the ultimate example of those who complain about the speck in someone's eye while they have planks in theirs.[38] They were well known for their bulging vocabularies and puffed-up talk, as with smooth words and flattering speech they tried to deceive the hearts of the simple.[39]

These Are

It's impossible to miss Jude's opinion (see APPENDIX 2) – and the Holy Spirit's, too, since the letter came by inspiration through a man moved by Him – but we notice another tripod, as three times over he says, *"These are"*[40]:

- Natural, but not spiritual;
- Divisive, not united;
- Living, but not alive in the Spirit; born, but not born again.

Jude could have concentrated on reminding believers of what they were, and we are thankful for scriptures that do this.

- *"You were slaves of sin, yet ... you were delivered."*[41]
- *"You were once darkness, but now you are light in the Lord."*[42]
- *"You were like sheep going astray, but have now returned to the shepherd and overseer of your souls."*[43]

Instead, he expressed what is true and exposed what was false by leaving both sides in no doubt about this very dark cloud – *"These are."*

MEETING HIM
Rom.14:10; 2 Cor.5:10

How shall I meet my Saviour's face
When He and I at last retrace
My works before His judgement seat,
My service laid down at His feet,
Will His 'Well done' make it complete?

How shall I meet my Saviour's eyes,
That fire which proves and purifies:
A searching, penetrating gaze
That estimates my words and ways,
Will they be worthy of His praise?

How shall I stand before His throne?
My eyes cast down before His own?
Or shall it be with gold, not dross;
With joy, not grief; with gain, not loss;
I trace the triumph of His cross?

My Lord, my Saviour, glorious King,
Help me today prepare to bring
Some gold, and silver, precious stones;
Some sacrifice that gladly owns
And proves Your sacrifice atones.

Oh, may I meet my Saviour's smile,
Cause Him who died to reconcile
To view a work that's all His own –
Not mine, but His, and for Him done –
Then from His hand receive a crown.
(A. McIlree)

6. BENEDICTION: ON THE BASIS OF 'WHERE?'

"But you, beloved, building yourselves up on your most holy faith, praying in the Holy Spirit, keep yourselves in the love of God, looking for the mercy of our Lord Jesus Christ unto eternal life. And on some have compassion making a distinction; but others save with fear, pulling them *out of the fire, hating even the garment defiled by the flesh"* (Jude vv.20-23).

* * *

It's three thousand years since Solomon wrote, *"Better is the end of a thing than its beginning."*[1] Jude's short message proves this to be true, and yet it's noticeable that if the letter could be bent around to form a circle the end would connect in remarkable relevance with the beginning. We needn't be surprised for the same could be done with the whole canon of Scripture. Bend the whole Book into a circle and we will find that the theme in the opening chapters of Genesis, the first man with his bride in the presence of the tree of life, finds its counterpart in the closing chapters of the Revelation with the second Man, His bride and the tree of life. This is the divine order of inspiration, so there's nothing accidental about it and Jude would be the first to become aware of this as he penned his part. It was no random collection of sayings, but something closely interconnected, so that its purpose would be recognised firstly by him, then by those who received it, and ultimately by us. What a pity it would be if in our day we missed the integration that is presented to us in its layout!

Having begun with a salutation, which led into thoughts of salvation and the need for contention, he then gave a resounding condemnation of false teachers who had crept in unnoticed and much-needed revelation to strengthen the faithful. This was Spirit-given that they might be enabled to contend and overcome, and then be encouraged by a benediction that contains shades of what he had already shared.

It's easy to see, when Jude comes to the close of his letter, that he has become very adept at moving his tripod. What began in verse 1 with thoughts of being called, beloved and preserved is reflected in the content of the benediction where they are still beloved and kept. He did well, as an effective helper, to allay their fears by showing that he had made the essential first step of grasping the reality of their situation. This was vital for he didn't want to leave them there, but to lift them above it and to assure them that they could be lifted above it. So he began his benediction by fixing their eyes on the Trinity – the Holy Spirit, God, and the Lord Jesus Christ – and kept their eyes there at its end. It was a wonderful way, like balm to the soul, to let them know that, in spite of all their difficulties, a united God combined Their ministry toward them. Of all Jude's tripods, this is the greatest: the divine

Tri-unity were working together for their blessing and comfort, which They sealed with a benediction that could be even more real to them than the hardships they faced.

It's interesting that the Holy Spirit is the first to be mentioned for there's a false notion that the Holy Spirit can be referred to as the third Person of deity. Deity has no third Person. In Matthew 28, we read about the Father, the Son and the Holy Spirit and it's this particular order that causes some to speak of the Lord Jesus as the second Person and the Holy Spirit as the third. Paul helps us to see this in the closing words of his second letter to Corinth: *"The grace of the Lord Jesus Christ, and the love of God, and the communion of the Holy Spirit be with you all. Amen."* We say "Amen" to the truth of this, and also to the order. He wasn't disagreeing with the Lord's order in Matthew 28 or suggesting that He is first, the Father second, and the Holy Spirit third. Like Jude, he was not inferring any descending order, but rather Their equality. Jude was speaking about how all three are inseparably concerned and involved in helping them overcome the difficulties in their company. Louis Berkhof is at pains to show that the terminology of Person in the Trinity is not completely satisfactory, as it suggests separate identity, and no one is in doubt that the Trinity is one in essence. He points out the conversation that can take place between Father, Son and Spirit, and how hypostasis led to the term existentia as distinct from essentia. The upshot is that the matter is too profound, and notions of priority are misplaced.

Beloved ... Beloved ... Beloved

It's interesting to note what he said at the opening of his letter: *"You are called, beloved, and preserved,"* so we find the word *"beloved"* in verse 1, again in verse 3 and finally in verse 20. So it's one of Jude's tripods. The thought of being *"beloved"* is first expressed in relation to God's care for this gathering, and the next three occurrences is Jude's concern and affection for them. He was sharing in the divine affections of God toward this gathering, and they would become very much aware of that as they read the letter. Jude felt for them what Paul expressed to the church in Philippi: *"God is my witness, how greatly I long for you all in the affection of Jesus Christ."*[2] How wonderful to feel as He feels and to love as He loves. Is it possible? The Lord Jesus says, *"As the Father loved Me, I also have loved you; abide in My love,"* and we abide or continue in it by showing it to Him and to others.

Building ... Praying ... Keeping

At the opening of the letter, we see what God does for them and for us, but verses 20 and 21 speak about *"building"* in regard to what we do for ourselves. By saying, *"But you, beloved, building yourselves up on your most holy faith, praying in the Holy Spirit,"* he was introducing two thoughts to them. One was the triumph of the Person within them, for he wants them to know that the Holy Spirit, the Father, and the Son are their only means of victory. They alone are the source of all triumph. Just as the Lord Jesus Christ has ensured our salvation, our service is ensured by all three Persons working together as They did at the cross. Now, from the throne of God He wants to make known to them that the reality of God's power and presence ought to be sensed within them.

The Father's care should be known within them, and the love of the Lord Jesus Christ ought to be ministering to their own spirit through the Holy Spirit. So he was saying that, first of all, it's the triumph of the triune Person within, but it's coupled with the thought of triumphing in the triune purpose. Jude had two reasons for saying *"building yourselves up in your most holy faith,"* for two things were happening in this gathering. One was they were being impeded by false men; and, secondly, they were wrestling with an inward impediment that was self-inflicted, as some of them yielded to the spiritual effects of false teaching. This was a gathering of the Lord's people who had known the blessing of God in their salvation and of being brought together through baptism and addition into the joy of assembly service. Then these men crept in to this unsuspecting company of disciples who probably had rejoiced in their coming, until they saw the effect they were having on one and another.

Jude became aware there was something far wrong and intended writing to them about common salvation, but he knew this would be hard to achieve since some were not saved at all. Others who were saved had their joy diminished because of the impact these false teachers were making. As he thought of the Person and the purpose having an effect on them, he saw this triplet as being the essence of their spiritual survival.

- Building themselves up through constant devotion to con-structive biblical teaching, which is the faith being lived by faith. It's not salvation followed by legislation; it's believing faith followed by faith in our beliefs;
- Praying in the Holy Spirit by maintaining a regular prayer life

that is Spirit-led;
- Keeping themselves in the love of God, living in it and being obedient to it by keeping His commandments.[3]

These must lie at the heart of every believer's service, if we want to be building ourselves up, to keep on praying, and to keep on keeping ourselves in His love. The tense of the Greek verbs indicates an on-going commitment, so we should be consistently building, praying and keeping rather than haphazard. If God is your Keeper[4],He will never let you go, and our response should confirm that we want to keep up our devotion and never let it go. God has laid a sure foundation in each believer, but the problem is that some have an unsure structure. What he has laid can never be taken away, but these men were doing their utmost to take away the satisfaction and joy from their service.

It's always the adversary's aim that, if he doesn't keep us from forgiveness in God's salvation, he will do all he can to keep us from fulfilment in godly service. His aim, of course, is not only to deprive the believer, but also to keep you from giving satisfaction to the heart of God. The secret lies in our wanting to do what God has already done. In verse 1, He is the One who keeps; and in verse 21 we keep ourselves. In both verses, the word is the same – *tēreō* – which means to guard by keeping your eye on it. He is our guardian and there should be a corresponding keeping desire in the hearts of those He is guarding. We should be protective of all He protects. What a challenge this is! Are we genuinely keeping our eyes on preserving our love for the Lord and for His Word?

The purpose of building, praying and keeping is not only for the good of the person, but for edifying the whole assembly. We should be making it an edifice of building, praying, loving people, but we can't be this without being men and women of the Word. Paul spoke about *"the word of His grace, which is able to build you up."*[5] He also taught us to *"pursue the things which make for peace and the things by which one may edify another."*[6] He also reminds us that *"love edifies,"*[7] so the assembly should be a place where sharing the Word and showing love provide the right atmosphere for spiritual enjoyment and growth.

During the years of Israel's wilderness journey, there were men who carried the ark of the LORD on their shoulders. This meant they walked closely together, and at the end of their sojourn they waited together. The ark is a symbol of the exalted Lord Jesus Christ keeping us together in step with each other in collective testimony. With Him, we walk and wait, and worship; so we can readily link our *"most holy faith"* with the Man in the Most Holy Place. Just as our most holy faith is for the enriching of our corporate walk, the Most Holy Place is for expressing our worship through our great High Priest as the most holy Person. Jude wanted to encourage his readers to walk with the Lord in such a way that their prayerful adherence to the Word would be clearly evident to those whose sole mission was to upset them. It was only by maintaining a close relationship with Him that they could contend earnestly for the faith. It was for them to take care of the earnestness, and they could leave the effectiveness with God.

On some ... Some ... Others

Damage had already been done in this gathering. Some had been influenced by the persuasive arguments of the false teachers, and their confidence had been shaken. This prompted Jude to make this Christlike appeal: *"on some have compassion."* Once again, he was asking them to do what God had done for them. He had shown "mercy," and His mercy should make them merciful. Now it was being multiplied to them, so they ought to be merciful to their damaged brothers and sisters. This should have made an impact on those who caused the damage, as they saw mercy being shown by those who disagreed with them for letting it happen.

Not all versions of the Bible clearly show who had been affected. The English Standard Version says, *"And have mercy on those who doubt; save others by snatching them out of the fire; to others show mercy with fear, hating even the garment stained by the flesh"*; and the Revised Version translates it as, *"And on some have mercy ... and some save ... and on some have mercy."* They have done this because the Greek word *hous*, which can be translated as "some" or "others," is used three times in these verses. This meant three kinds of targeted help:

- The first was by showing mercy to those who were wavering, which allowed them to put God's mercy to good use, while causing them to enjoy the Lord's promise: *"Blessed are the merciful, for they shall obtain mercy"*[8];
- The second were those who needed to be forcibly hauled from the fire of heretical teaching. They had listened to false men, had played with fire, and needed strong hands to bring robust deliverance;
- The third needed mercy combined with a sense of alarm that those with a stained testimony, depicted by filthy garments, could defile those who were trying to help.

Their defilement didn't come from external staining that marred their outer garment, but from fleshly desires in the person that stained their inner garment (Gr. *chitōn*). When the Lord looked at the church in Sardis, He said, *"You have a few names ... who have not defiled their garments,"*[9] and He meant they had been blackened. His word to Laodicea was, *"I counsel you to buy from Me ... white garments,"*[10] so that they would stand out as being different. In other words, He wanted their testimony to be pure. Laodicea was well known for its flocks of black sheep from which black clothing was made, but the church should be well known for the whiteness of its purity.

Verse 22 shows that the damaged Christians could be seen in three different parts: those who were not seriously affected, those who were, and those who could defile anyone who tried to rescue them. Jude must have known there was a fourth part who remained faithful and that they were to be the rescuers. They had a big task, didn't they? All three approaches may still be called for in trying to rescue Christian lives from various kinds of damage. For some, being merciful will be enough; for others, it may take a firmer hand; and for some, it may be with fear that we try to win them back knowing that, being damaged, they may damage those who are trying to help. It's not enough to be well meaning in any of these. Each approach is different, but mercy and strength and fear are essential elements of Spirit-given help.

Trying to assist spiritual recovery is impossible without doing it in a spiritual way. We may know some who have been side-tracked. If so, what has been our response? Critical, judgemental or merciful? When Jude began by saying, *"Mercy, peace, and love be multiplied to you,"* he knew how much these would be needed in the recovery process. It was as if he were assuring them that, if they wanted to win their brothers and sisters, they should make sure that what they were receiving from God was what they were conveying to them.

There's a remarkable illustration of this in the days of King Jehoash in 2 Kings 12 when Jehoiada was priest. The temple had fallen into disrepair and there were obvious areas of damage that called for reinvestment and restoration. They needed to give in a very definite way for the renewal that some parts required and Jehoiada came up with an idea that had never been thought of before. He took a box, bored a hole in its lid, and set it beside the altar of God for collections that would go toward restoring damaged stones and woodwork. Things were not as they should be, but a young king and a priest found a way of giving the people a collective sense of responsibility and purpose.

With no precedent to follow, Jehoiada could have placed his box in a number of places, and we would have understood if he had set it at the gate of the temple. He chose the altar, the place of sacrifice, that pointed to the cross-work of the Lord Jesus Christ where He offered Himself for sin and for our common salvation. He even chose its north side, which in Hebrew means dark, gloomy and hidden, where the lamb was slain.[11] It's a very interesting thought that Jehoiada and the people knew that investing in the temple of God began at the altar of God, and we can apply the same principle. Those who share the temple character of a local assembly[12] also understand that their desire to invest in the people of God begins with our appreciation of the cross.

Does this hold a valuable lesson for us? Are we not aware of brothers and sisters who are like damaged stones and are badly in need of help? To what extent are we investing in the ministry of restoration? Thankfully it's not often that we have to talk with a brother or sister who is leaving the church or has to be removed from it, but in that conversation it's important that we discuss the Lord's provision of a way back. Even in a time of disappointment or disagreement, we need to start there so that their affections are won all over again by the man of Calvary. It's at that stage they need to know how they will restore their relationship with the Lord and restart building themselves up in their most holy faith.

This implies three things: willing acceptance of His teaching, consistent adherence to upholding it, and heartfelt allegiance. It also implies absorbing it, understanding it, and living by it in such a way that our manner of living is affected and conditioned by it. Jude's phrase is very meaningful for it really means that *"the faith"* of verse 3 has become *"your faith."* More than that, it means that *"the most holy faith"* has become our *"most holy faith,"* and this implies that its nature becomes ours. Yes, we know that God's truths are our guidelines for spiritual service, but they need to be more than that. They need to be our guidelines for spiritual character. His *most holy* faith should produce holiness, and His most holy *faith* should produce faithfulness. If so, the real impact of His teaching will be seen in the holiness of our faithfulness, and in the faithfulness of our holiness.

Sadly, some believers seem to believe that doctrine gets in the way of Christian living, without realising how essential it is. Paul made it clear to Timothy that doctrine accords with godliness,[13] so the doctrines of *"the faith"* produce holiness, faithfulness and godliness. Our goal, as individuals and as churches, is to permit and assist this Spirit-given discovery, and to help those who have fallen to discover it too. It's not only restoring them to faith; it's helping them to walk in the holiness of the faith, so that the joy of their salvation and service may be restored. There is nothing more powerful than holiness, yet there are Christians all over the world who are praying for power. We might pray for power and never grow in holiness, but if we pray and grow in holiness we definitely will grow in power. We need an overwhelming sense of the holiness of God to accompany all that we are individually and collectively. It will monitor our character and conduct; how we stand before a holy God, and allow others to see *"how holily and righteously and unblameably we behaved"*[14] toward them.

This is the kind of ministry Jude was thinking of as he surveyed a damaged gathering and its need for repair. He was the Jehoiada of his day appealing for restorers on behalf of his King, and yet he knew that what he called *"our common salvation"* wasn't common to all. False teachers had never *"begun in the Spirit,"*[15] so they couldn't continue in the Spirit; they also had no faith and no holiness. But there were others who started in the Spirit, and were not being made perfect in the Spirit. They had faith, but were not serving in the holiness of the faith. They had been affected by the adversary, conflicting thoughts were going on in their minds and hearts, and Jude had good reason to be concerned.

NOTHING BUT LEAVES
Matthew 21:19

He looked before He faced the cross
On a fig tree full and fair,
But the very thing He looked for most
Was the thing it did not bear.
And, in spite of all His mercy shown,
In spite of a heart that grieves,
It never turned from its fruitless ways
And gave Him "nothing but leaves."

He had traced their walk from early days,
In the call to Abraham;
He had seen their bondage overcome
By blood from the Passover lamb.
And the path God chose for His redeemed,
The chosen whom He receives,
They chose to despise His Lamb and Man,
And gave Him "nothing but leaves."

He looked on us as He bore His cross
With a longing still the same,
That those who claim to own His grace
Will honour and praise His Name
By showing the love we have for Him,
And the faith by which each cleaves.
Will we spend our days in fruitful growth
Or give Him – "nothing but leaves"?
(A. McIlree)

7. DOXOLOGY: ON THE BASIS OF 'WHOM?'

"Now to Him who is able to keep you from stumbling, and to present you faultless before the presence of His glory with exceeding joy, to God our Saviour, Who alone is wise, be glory and majesty, dominion and power, both now and forever. Amen" (Jude vv.24,25).

* * *

God always initiates His own rescue missions. He did it in Genesis 3 in His call to fallen Adam and Eve, He did it through the cross of the Lord Jesus Christ to provide the only means of calling fallen sinners to Himself, and Jude's doxology leaves us in no doubt that, in spite of his readers' present struggles, God would do it for them too. He began his short letter in the heights of the promise of the gospel, which assured them that they were called, beloved and preserved, and he ends by bringing them to greater heights in the prospect of glory.

Two verses capture the first for us, and the last two verses capture the second. Victory condensed in four short verses! In the mid-section of 21 verses lies an inspired message that deals with the heat of the battle, the darkness of the enemy, the deceit of false teachers, but not the defeat of the believer. The overall message that would be reinforced as the letter was read and re-read, was they were going from victory to victory, from the Victor being with them to them being with the Victor.

> His be the Victor's name
> Who fought the fight alone;
> Triumphant saints no honour claim,
> Their conquest was His own.
> *(Samuel Gandy)*

To Him Who is Able

Divine ability is unique, and each believer is assured of it through the power that God has demonstrated in the gospel. Eternal security is guaranteed. The means of saving grace was seen when the Victor of the cross *"offered up prayers and supplications ... to Him who was able to save Him from* [Gr. *ek* – out of] *death,"*[1] and the end is seen in His being *"able to keep."* The first has underwritten the triumph of the Saviour, and the second underlines the triumph of the saved. Both are integral to *"our common salvation,"* and every born-again believer is secure. The nature of the gospel confirms God's ability, and the word *dunamai* supports the certainty of the power Jude speaks of in his doxology. The same word is used in Paul's doxology in Romans 16:25,[2] and we also find it in Mark 2:7 where the scribes asked, *"Who can forgive sins?"* The word *dunamai* means they put a question over the Lord's deity by asking, *"Who is able to forgive sins but God alone?"*

97

During the time of captivity in Babylon, when Daniel was cast into the lions' den, King Darius spent a sleepless night before rushing to find out in the morning if he had survived. As soon as he arrived, *"he cried out with a lamenting voice ... 'Daniel, servant of the living God, has your God, whom you serve continually, been able to deliver you from the lions?'"*[3] To his relief, Daniel was unharmed and replied, *"O king, live forever! My God sent His angel and shut the lions' mouths, so that they have not hurt me."* His faith in God hadn't wavered, and he was living proof that *"our God whom we serve is able to deliver."*[4] Like Daniel, Jude never doubted God's ability, and he would know that the God who shut the mouths of lions was just as able to shut the mouths of false teachers who were like wolves in sheep's clothing.[5]

To Keep You From Stumbling

Job called God *"the watcher of men,"*[6] and evidently trusted Him as his guardian and protector. So can we, for He hasn't changed. David knew this and pre-dated Jude by putting the words *"keep"* and *"preserve"* into the same verse when he wrote, *"You shall keep them, You shall preserve them."*[7] There's no doubt at all that God is able to keep His saints from tripping, in that He is able to deliver us *"out of"* them, but Jude's point is that God is able to keep us from going into them. What tremendous comfort this must have been to those who had been stumbled, and to us whenever we stumble too! His readers faced major obstacles for, apart from anything in their lives that could cause them to stumble, they had false teachers who were set on tripping them.

God can keep us from falling, from tripping and being tripped. Many a child of God lives with deep regret about falling into sin, and some never get over it. Memories of old failures can be an effective weapon in the hands of the adversary, and he's very good at raking up the past. If this is something you wrestle with, let God take it from you once and for all. He knows how the adversary uses these things to prevent us from knowing the peace and joy of His forgiveness, and the satisfaction of spiritual progress. We may even rake them up ourselves, but, once repented of and forgiven, He never will. His caring hand would rather erase such disturbing thoughts and help us to say, *"Do not rejoice over me, my enemy; when I fall, I will arise."*[8] God, in His mercy, gives a way of escape, and wants to remind us that there is a way back up when we fall.

It's also true, of course, that He cautions us, *"let him who thinks he stands take heed lest he fall."*[9] We need to be very careful that assuming we are above falling doesn't become the very thing that brings us down! Peter assures us that we *"are kept by the power of God"*[10]; Paul tells us that we are *"eagerly waiting for the revelation of our Lord Jesus Christ, who will confirm you to the end, that you may be blameless in the day of our Lord Jesus Christ."*[11] We are kept, are being kept, and always will be kept by our triune God.

To Present You Faultless

For false teachers to hear this promise being given to genuine believers resembles the position Judas was in when he heard some of the Lord's ministry in the Upper Room and had his feet washed without being *"completely clean."*[12] There's a big difference between being false and being faulty. It may be as you read this that you automatically think how your own faults have kept you from full involvement and enjoyment in your service for the Lord, and this may have led to feelings of inadequacy. God knows all about our faults and is well able to help us. In fact, He can do more with inferiority than He can with superiority. The superiority complex needs to be broken by Him, but He graciously reshapes any feelings of inferiority. None of us is adequate, and it wouldn't be a healthy sign if any Christian ever claimed to be.

All believers have faults, but all will be faultless on the day when we appear in His presence above. The struggle with sin will be over, and so will its stains for we will be, as the Greek says, *"amōmos"* – without blemish and blameless. Christlike, at last! He Himself will present us there. There will be nothing in us to displease Him, nothing to disappoint us, and nothing the adversary can defend. He was defeated at the cross[13] and will be again when everyone in *"the church, which is His body"*[14] – in the building, the body and the bride – stands perfected at His throne!

Before the Presence of His Glory

We began faith's journey by standing *before* Him in our guilt at the cross; we continue our service *for* Him by standing in his grace;[15] and we will finish our service by standing *with* Him in His glory. We are being taken from the grief of the cross to the glory of the throne. What a transformation! When we are raised at His coming, Christ will present (Gr. *paristēmi*) the church to Himself, and this means we will stand beside Him as a bride with her Bridegroom. We will be *"before the presence"* (Gr. *katenōpion*) of God, which means we will stand directly in front of Him as His Son presents the church to Himself, and we will have bodies that are like *"the body of His glory."*[16]

Some versions say, *"His glorious body,"* but the word is a noun, not an adjective, so in bodies like *"the body of His glory,"* we will stand *"before the presence of His glory."* We also know that great men of God in Old and New Testament days were deeply affected by the glory of God. In their earthly experience, some feared[17] and fell,[18] but, when the church enjoys her heavenly experience, the bride will stand. More than that, there will be *"exceeding joy"* (Gr. *agalliasis*).

The meaning of this was first expressed when Elizabeth heard Mary's voice and explained how *"the babe leaped in my womb for joy."*[19] John the Baptist was as yet unborn, but not unmoved. Peter captured its meaning in his first letter when he spoke of those who *"greatly rejoice"* (Gr. *agalliao*) in the anticipation of what is yet to be revealed at the Lord's coming. Later, he used the same word when referring to *"exceeding joy."*[20] The root thought means to jump for joy and, like John the Baptist, the lame man in Acts 3:8 was *"leaping"* as he entered the Temple praising God. Both are linked to unrestrained joy, and the same applies to the resurrected, glorified members of the church, which is His body. In their new bodies, with unlimited and uninhibited joy, there will be a sense of jumping for joy.

To God Our Saviour

Many versions translate this verse as, *"To the only God, our Saviour, through Jesus Christ our Lord, be glory, majesty, dominion, and authority, before all time and now and forever. Amen.*[21]

Be Glory

The glory (Gr. *doxa*: honour, praise, worship) of God consists of all the attributes of His character that radiate from Him in the full harmony of His Being. *"Through Jesus Christ"* indicates that He also is the brightness and outshining of God's glory.[22] The whole character of Deity has been made known through Him by means of His incarnation, ministry on earth, His death and resurrection. He is the only means by which the glory of God has been brought to us in the gospel, and the only means by which we are being brought to the glory of God.

Majesty

This refers to God in the greatness of His sovereignty, and Peter uses the related word *megaleiotēs* to express the magnificence, superbness, and splendour that belong to the perfection of God and His Son. We see God as *"the Majesty on high"* in Hebrews 1:3, and in chapter 8:1, with the Lord Jesus Christ at His side as co-equal in His majesty.[23]

There's a wonderful recognition of this at the beginning of Psalm 104 where the psalmist says, *"Bless the LORD, O my soul! O LORD my God, You are very great: You are clothed with honour and majesty, who cover Yourself with light as with a garment."* It's interesting to note that his words for *"clothed"* and *"cover"* convey the thought of being wrapped, and we can easily relate this to the Infant Jesus being *"wrapped in swaddling cloths"*[24] and then as a Man being *"wrapped"* in linen for burial.[25] When He came to earth in His birth, and was ready to leave it through His death, His wrapping followed the size and contours of His frame, but how is the eternal God wrapped with honour, majesty and light? The question becomes even more interesting when we discover that the word for "garment" (*kasalmāh* from *salmāh* and *simlāh*) means "a dress that takes shape from what is under it."

The psalmist was speaking of God's pre-bodily form probably around a thousand years before the Saviour came, so he wasn't thinking of a garment taking shape from His body, but from His Being. His ministry and miracles were shaped by His nature and followed the content and contours of One who is in the form of God.[26] One hymn-writer says, "Through this dark vale of sorrow, He clothed with pity went," and he, too, was thinking of the clothing of His Being. When the woman touched the hem of His garment, she wasn't healed because there was something magical in the garment that covered His body. She drew power *"out of Him"* for she had reached far beyond the fringe of what covered His body to the garment that was shaped by the majesty of his inner Being.

Compassion is an attribute of Deity and Jesus showed it when He was on earth, in the same way as He caused people to see and hear the evidence of His omniscience, omnipotence, love and grace, which with all His other attributes, caused some to recognise Him as God manifested in the flesh. In all that He did through His bodily presence, the honour, majesty, and light of His inner Being shone out. When He said, *"I am the light of the world,"*[27] He was speaking as the eternal Being, co-equal with His God and Father, *"the brightness of His glory"*[28] and of the outshining of divine light from His nature. Through Him, and through the gospel, *"The light shines in the darkness,"*[29] and still takes shape from the nature of the *"I AM"*. No wonder Job said, *"He is unique, and who can make*

Him change?"[30] Hallelujah! What a Saviour!

Isaiah's words in Isaiah 61:10 are like an echo of the psalmist, for they both spoke of the harmony between *"my soul"* and *"my God"*; and this helps us to see that our inner being is capable of blessing and rejoicing as it meditates on God. They give us real insight to the connection and communication between our inner being and His, just as we find them in Romans 8:16 where we read that, *"The Spirit Himself bears witness with our spirit that we are children of God."* From deep within our own being, we *"bless"* God, and the word *bār*ᵉ*chiy* conveys an attitude of kneeling down before Him in adoration. We sense how He is "clothed" (*lābāsh*ᵉ*tā* from *lābash*), and as we apply Isaiah 61:10 to our own experience, He sees how we are clothed (*hilbiyshaniy* from *lābash*). The same thought is used of Him and of the redeemed, and we can take the lesson that, if His garment takes shape from what is underneath, so should ours for we have been "clothed" by Him. This will help others to see Christ in us and that we are "wrapped" up in Him!

> Let the beauty of Jesus be seen in me,
> All His wondrous compassion and purity;
> O Thou Spirit divine, all my nature refine
> 'Till the beauty of Jesus be seen in me.
> *(Albert Orsborn)*

Dominion

God's overall dominion is seen right at the beginning of our Bibles when we read what He said in Genesis 1:26, *"Let Us make man in Our image, according to Our likeness; let them have dominion ..."* By delegating dominion the Trinity showed Their own, but the day is coming when the Lord will come in His majesty. *"He shall speak peace to the nations; His dominion shall be 'from sea to sea, and from the River to the ends of the earth.'"*[31]

Power

This is the inherent power of Deity that is seen in God's control and authority over times and seasons,[32] in the Son's right to forgive sins,[33] and to give the great commission.[34] The same word is used in Luke 23:7 where Pilate heard that Jesus belonged to Herod's "jurisdiction" and sent Him to Herod. Well might we say that He didn't belong to the jurisdiction of *"that fox,"*[35] but that the fox was under the jurisdiction of the Lamb! Having authority in heaven and on earth, the Lord's jurisdiction is much wider, and God *"will judge the world in righteousness by the Man whom He has ordained."*[36]

Both Now and Forever

The Greek phrase at the end of this verse falls into three parts of Jude's final tripod:

- *pro pantos tou aiōnos* – before all time;
- *kai nun* – and now;
- *eis pantas tous aiōnas* – and forever. Amen.

With these words, Jude completed his letter by emphasising that the Son is co-equal with the Father and co-eternal, and that the redeemed will be gathered Home. It is very evident that his benediction reinforced Christ's true nature to those who knew

Him as their Lord and Saviour, while delivering a rebuke to the false teachers who were guilty of *"denying our only Master and Lord, Jesus Christ"* (Jude 1:4, RV).

DOXOLOGIES

In the New Testament, Paul, Peter, John and Jude introduce a doxology at different stages of their letters: sometimes, at the end; at other times, part way through. It is good for us to see that these are not interchangeable or random outbursts of praise to God, but rather meaningful exaltation with phrases that relate to the context. For instance, in Romans we find one at the end of eleven carefully reasoned chapters of gospel truth that led from the depravity of man, through the fundamental doctrines of grace, to the complete certainty of salvation provided by a sovereign God.

Paul is so masterly in his reasoning that we could stand in awe of his lawyer-like wisdom, and of how he concluded his whole presentation with a doxology that ascribes everything to the all-wise, all-knowing God who needed no assistance from angels or men. The wording of the doxology is perfectly suited to the redeemed giving glory to God for the wonder of His ways revealed in the Son and His ways. With a timely outburst of praise, he exclaims:

"Oh, the depth of the riches both of the wisdom and knowledge of God! How unsearchable are His judgements and His ways past finding out! For who has known the mind of the Lord? Or who has become His counsellor? Or who has first given to Him and it shall be repaid to him? For of Him and

through Him and to Him are *all things, to whom* be *glory forever. Amen."*[37]

As the road south from Colorado reaches the border with New Mexico, the western horizon is filled by a magnificent view of the Southern Rocky Mountains. Their snow-capped peaks glow red in the sunset, and they are appropriately known as the Sangre de Cristo range, which means the blood of Christ. They are like a visual reminder of their spiritual counterpart in these eleven chapters in Romans. Paul lifts our eyes to focus on another range of mountain peaks that show what the precious blood of Christ has achieved. Well might we feast on lofty thoughts of how it has secured propitiation that satisfies the holiness of God and prevents His wrath being shown to everyone who believes; and absorb the marvel of how it also secures redemption that overcomes the sinfulness of the sinner. As we take in the heights presented in the great truths of the gospel, we also are led to repeat Paul's doxological song.

The relevance of a doxology is seen again at the end of chapter 16, which brings an end to the application of the first eleven chapters through the surrender and submission of the Christian's life. The opening appeal in chapter 12 – *"I beseech you therefore, brethren, by the mercies of God, that you present your bodies a living sacrifice ..."* – follows the doxology at the end of chapter 11 and precedes the unveiling of practical truth relating to spiritual gifts and other aspects of Christian service.

How could we ever stand at the end of these eleven chapters that are so filled with the wonder of the gospel and not be moved by this appeal?

But we never can prove
The delights of His love,
Until all on the altar we lay;
For the favour He shows,
And the joy He bestows,
Are for them who will trust and obey.
(*John H. Sammis*)

The appeal leads into aspects of obedience that are to be shown by our conduct in the world and in the churches, and on into the appropriateness of the closing doxology:

"Now to Him who is able to establish you according to my gospel and the preaching of Jesus Christ, according to the revelation of the mystery kept secret since the world began but now has been made manifest, and by the prophetic Scriptures has been made known to all nations, according to the commandment of the everlasting God, for obedience to the faith—to God, alone wise, be glory through Jesus Christ forever. Amen."[38]

Another example is found in Paul's letter to the Ephesians. Right from his opening, we are lifted up to adore the One who *"has blessed us with every spiritual blessing in the heavenly places in Christ,"* and then we are introduced to how He has done this through His electing love, sharing His holiness, predestination, redemption, forgiveness, the mystery of His will, summing up all things in Christ, and guaranteeing our eternal inheritance. As in Romans, Paul applies body teaching in chapters 2 and 3 to our spiritual service before returning to the subject of spiritual gifts in chapter 4. In a nutshell, his message is that the blessings and character of *"the church, which is His body"*[39] should be seen in the churches, and this is crystallised in the doxology that follows. *"Now to Him who is able to do exceedingly abundantly above all that we ask or think, according to the power that works in us, to Him be glory in the church by Christ Jesus to all generations, forever and ever. Amen."*[40]

Jude's doxology is no less relevant to what he has been saying. Tripping and fault-finding were everyday realities among his readers, and he systematically addressed the hazards of their outlook in verses 1-23 before fixing their up-look in verses 24 and 25. What a contrast! He also set out to lift their spirits by reasserting the Saviour's rightful role, which the false teachers denied; and the fourfold character of His rightful place, which they despised (in v.8, dignitaries is Gr. *doxa* = glory). For himself as the writer, his closing benediction complemented and confirmed his opening salutation. It comforted his brothers and sisters and assured him, the boy from the same Nazareth home as the Saviour, that the servant also will be safe Home with his Master. Having followed his careful handling of scriptural truth and spiritual trials, we come to the end of his short and powerful letter and are ready to say as he did:

"Now to Him who is able to keep you from stumbling and to present you blameless before the presence of his glory with great joy, to the only God, our Saviour, through Jesus Christ our Lord, be glory, majesty, dominion, and authority, before all time and now and forever. Amen." [41]

TO HIM WHO IS ABLE

To Him who is able
To keep us – His called ones,
Preserved in Christ Jesus,
The saints of the Father –
To keep us from falling,
And faultless to set us
Before His bright glory
With fulness of joy.

To the Lord God, who keepeth
Midst sin and in weakness,
Whose wisdom alone is,
To God and our Saviour
Be majesty, glory,
Dominion and power,
Both now and for ever
Amen, Amen.
(Naylor)

REFERENCES

CHAPTER ONE: SALUTATION

(1) Acts 1:14 (2) Jn 15:20 (3) Matt.10:36 (4) Eph.4:10 (5) Lk.2:41-50 (6) Jer.18:18,RV (7) Phil.2:7 (8) 1 Pet.2:23 NIV (9) Matt.8:20 (10) The House of Christmas (11) Jas.1:17 (12) Jn. 1:46 (13) 1 Cor 2:8 (14) Phil. 2:7 (15) 1 Kin.8:27 (16) Ex.12:4 (17) 1 Cor.15:5-7 (18) Jn 14:22 (19) Jn 7:3-5 (20) Rom.11:34 (21) Jas.1:1; 2:1 (22) Mk.8:31 (23) Jn 9:4 (24) Acts 2:42 (25) Ps.55:22 (26) Lk.21:25 (27) Jn 15:19 (28) Ps.29:4 (29) Jas.1:18; 1 Pet.1:23 (30) Rom.5:6 ESV (31) Eph.2:5 (32) Eph.2:3; 5:8 (33) Phil.3:14, RV; 2 Tim.1:9; Heb.3:1 (34) Ps.32:8 (35) Prov.15:3 (36) Heb.4:13 (37) 2 Pet.1:1 (38) 2 Thess.1:5 (39) Rom.2:5

CHAPTER TWO: SALVATION

(1) 2 Cor.11:4 (2) 2 Thess.2:3,8 (3) 1 Jn. 2:18,22; 4:3 (4) 2 Thess.2:6,7 (5) 2 Thess.2:10 (6) Rom.1:1,9,16 (7) Rom.8:21 (8) Gal.5:1 (9) Mal.3:6 (10) Heb.13:8 (11) 1 Tim.1:10 (12) 2 Tim.1:13 (13) Job 13:7 (14) Isa.40:12 (15) Isa.52:7 (16) Rom.10:15, RV (17) 1 Thess.1:5 (18) 1 Cor.1:17 (19) Gal.1:10 (20) Job 13:7, RV (21) 1 Cor.9:22 (22) Gal.3:1 (23) Gal.2:20 (24) 1 Tim.3:16 (25) Col.1:13 (26) 1 Cor.9:23 (27) 2 Cor.5:20 (28) Jn 6:27 (29) Matt.28:19,20 (30) 1 Pet.1:2 (31)

Matt.26:39; Mk.14:35 (32) Mk.1:19 (33) Prov.9:1 (34) Phil.1:27; Col.1:5,23

CHAPTER THREE: CONTENTION

(1) 2 Cor.4:13-18 (2) Acts 15:28 (3) Acts 15:25 (4) Rom.15:30 (5) Phlm.8,9 (6) 1 Tim.6:12, RV (7) 2 Cor.4:8,9 (8) MacArthur Commentary on 2 Corinthians (9) Matt.28:18-20 (10) Oxford Dictionaries (11) 2 Tim.4:3 (12) 2 Tim.1:13 (13) Tit.1:13 (14) Tit.1:7-9 (15) 2 Tim.4:7 (16) 2 Thess.2:15

CHAPTER FOUR: CONDEMNATION

(1) 2 Cor.11; 23-28 (2) Isa.29:15; Jer.17:9,10; Ezek.11:5 (3) Mk.14:57 (4) Rom.5:6 (5) 2 Pet.3:7 (6) Matt.10:16 (7) Jn.15:20 (8) 1 Pet.2:23, NIV; Matt.10:16 (9) Lev.1:14 (10) Songs 5:12 (11) Matt.7:15 (12) Zeph.3:3 (13) Neh.4:3 (14) Ruth 2:20 (15) Neh.13:4,5 (16) Acts 20:29 (17) Matt.7:16 (18) 1 Tim.6:5 (19) Rom.1:25, KJV (20) Mk.8:29 (21) 1 Jn 1:3 (22) Phil.1:7 (23) 2 Pet.1:4 (24) Heb.4:2 (25) Gen.4:10 (26) Heb.11:6 (27) Ps.51:14 (28) Jn 12:6 (29) 2 Kin.5:20-27 (30) Num.22:7 (31) 2 Pet.2:15 (32) Prov.18:16 (33) Ex.23:8 (34) Mic.3:11; 7:3 (35) Num.16:39-50 (36) Isa.57:20,21 (37) Matt.10:26; see Job 28:11 (38) Ps.92:13 (39) Ecc.11:3 (40) Prov.25:14 (41) Isa.40:26 (42) Phil.2:15 (43) Dan.12:3

CHAPTER FIVE: REVELATION

(1) Jer.49:8,30, RV (2) Prov.14:34 (3) Lev.20:17 (4) 1 Pet.2:23 (5) Ex.14:13 (6) Deut.25:18,19 (7) Num.23:19 (8) Ps.90:7,9 (9) Job 38:7 (10) Heb.12:22 (11) Gen.28:12; Mk.8:38, 13:27; 2 Thess.1:7; 1 Tim.5:21 (12) Ps.104:4; Heb.1:7 (13) Heb.1:14 (14) 1 Pet.1:5 (15) Lk.10:18 (16) Eph.6:11,12 (17) 2 Pet.2,4 (18) Gen.13:10 (19) Gen.19:28 (20) Deut.29:23 (21) Ps.95:11; Heb.3:11,16-19 (22) Jn 8:44 (23) 2 Pet.1:4 (24) Jn 1:12; Heb.3:1,2; Jude 14; 2 Cor.10:4; 1 Pet.1:2 (25) 1 Cor.3:9 RVM (26) 2 Tim.3:8 (27) Josh.1:2; Ex.33:11 (28) 1 Cor.1:18; Col.1:13 (29) 2 Chr.20:12 (30) Eph.6:11,13; Jas.4:7; 2 Cor.6:7 (31) Heb.2:14; 1 Jn 3:8 (32) Zech.3:2 (33) 1 Cor.2:11-14 (34) Gen.5:21-24 (35) 2 Pet.2:5 (36) 2 Thess.1:7-10 (37) Jude 8,10,16,18 (38) Matt.7:3 (39) Rom.16:18 (40) Jude vv.12,16,19 (41) Rom.6:17 (42) Eph.5:8 (43) 1 Pet.2:25

CHAPTER SIX: BENEDICTION

(1) Ecc.7:8, ESV (2) Phil.1:8 (3) Jn 15:9,10 (4) Ps.121:5 (5) Acts 20:32 (6) Rom.14:19 (7) 1 Cor.8:1 (8) Matt.5:7 (9) Rev.3:4 (10) Rev.3:18 (11) Lev.1:10,11; 4:33 (12) 1 Cor.3:17 (13) 1 Tim.6:3 (14) 1 Thess.2:10, RV (15) Gal.3:3

CHAPTER SEVEN: DOXOLOGY

(1) Heb.5:7 (2) See also Rom.1:16; 1 Cor.1:18; Eph.3:20 (3) Dan.6:20,21 (4) Dan.3:17 (5) Mat.7:15 (6) Job 7:20 (7) Ps.12:7 (8) Mic.7:8 (9) 1 Cor.10:12 (10) 1 Pet.1:5 (11) 1 Cor.1:7,8 (12) Jn. 13:10 (13) Heb.2:14; 1 Jn. 3:8 (14) Eph.1:22,23 (15) Rom.5:2 (16) Phil.3:21

(17) Isa.6:5; Lk.9:34 (18) Ezek.1:28; Matt.17:6; Rev.1:17 (19) Lk.1:44 (20) 1 Pet.1:6, 4:13 (21) ESV, NASB, NRSV, RSV; ASV, NIV & RV are substantially the same (22) Heb.1:3 (23) 2 Pet.1:16 (24) Lk.2:7 (25) Lk.23:53 (26) Phil.2:6 (27) Jn 8:12 (28) Heb.1:3 (29) Jn 1:5; 2 Cor.4:4,6 (30) Job 23:13 (31) Zech.9:10 (32) Acts 1:7 (33) Matt.9:6 (34) Matt.28:18-20 (35) Lk.13:32 (36) Acts 17:31 (37) Rom.11:33-36 (38) Rom.16:25-27 (39) Eph.1:22, 23 (40) Eph.3;20,21 (41) Jude v.25, ESV

APPENDIX 1 – JUDE'S TRIPODS

1. Called, beloved, and preserved – v.1
2. Preserved (Gr. *tēreō*), keep (Gr. *tēreō*), keep (Gr. *phulasso*: keep) – vv.1,21,24
3. Mercy, peace and love – v.2
4. Mercy (Gr. *eleos*), mercy (Gr. *eleos*), compassion (Gr. *eleeō*: mercy) – vv.2,21,22
5. Beloved by Jude – vv.3,17,20
6. Marked out for condemnation – v.4. Turn the grace of God into lewdness, Deny the only Master and Lord, Jesus Christ
7. Lord, God and Saviour – vv.4, 25
8. The people, angels, Sodom and Gomorrah – vv.5-7
9. Defile the flesh, reject authority, and speak evil of dignitaries – v.8
10. Cain, Balaam and Korah – v.11
11. Rocks and waves, shepherds and trees, clouds and stars – vv.12,13
12. These are – vv.12,16,19
13. Sensual, cause divisions, not having the Spirit– v.19
14. Building, praying, keeping – as we wait – v.20
15. The Holy Spirit, the love of God, our Lord Jesus Christ – vv.20,21
16. On some (Gr. *hous*: others) have compassion – v. 22, 23,

Some (Gr. *hous*) save out of the fire, Others (Gr. *hous*) detesting their defiled garments

17. Presented – faultless (v.24) – before His glory – with exceeding joy

18. Before all time (Gr. *pro pantos tou aiōnos*) – v. 25, and now (*kai nun*), and forever (Gr. *eis pantas*)

APPENDIX 2 – THE CHARACTER OF FALSE MEN

v.4

Crept in unnoticed; Marked out for this condemnation;
Ungodly men, who pervert the grace of our God into
sensuality (ESV);
Deny our only Master and Lord, Jesus Christ (ESV).

v.8

These dreamers defile the flesh;
Reject authority; Speak evil of dignitaries.

v.10

Speak evil of whatever they do not know;
and whatever they know naturally;
Like brute beasts, in these things they corrupt themselves.

v.11

They have gone in the way of Cain;
Have run greedily in the error of Balaam for profit;
Perished in the rebellion of Korah.

v.12

These are rocks (spots) in your love feasts;

They feast with you without fear;
Shepherding (serving) *only* themselves;
They are clouds without water, carried about by the winds;
Late autumn trees without fruit, twice dead, pulled up by
the roots.

v.13

Raging waves of the sea, foaming up their own shame;
Wandering stars for whom is reserved the blackness of darkness
forever.

v.15

To convict all who are ungodly ... their ungodly deeds ...
committed in an ungodly way, and of all the harsh things
which ungodly sinners have spoken against Him.

v.16

These are grumblers, complainers;
Walking according to their own lusts;
They mouth great swelling *words*, flattering people to gain
advantage.

v.18

Mockers ... who would walk according to their own ungodly lusts.

v.19

These are sensual persons, who cause divisions, not having the
Spirit.

WHAT THINK YE OF CHRIST?

What think ye of Christ? is the test
To try both your state and your scheme;
You cannot be right in the rest,
Unless you think rightly of Him;
As Jesus appears in your view,
As He is beloved or not,
So God is disposed to you,
And mercy, or wrath are your lot.

Some take Him a creature to be,
A man, or an angel at most:
Sure these have not feelings like me,
Nor know themselves wretched, and lost;
So guilty, so helpless, am I,
I durst not confide in His blood;
Nor on His protection rely,
Unless I were sure he is God.

Some call Him a Saviour in word,
But mix their own works with their plan;
And hope He His help will afford,
When they have done all that they can;
If sayings prove rather too light,
(A little they own they may fail)
They purpose to make up full weight,
By casting his name in the scale.

If asked what of Jesus I think,
Although my best thoughts are but poor;
I say He's my meat and my drink,
My life, and my strength, and my store,
My Shepherd, my husband, my friend,
My Saviour from sin, and from thrall,
My hope from beginning to end,
My portion, my Lord, and my all.
(John Newton)

ABOUT THE AUTHOR

Andy was born in Glasgow, Scotland, He came to know the Lord in 1954, and was baptized in 1958. He is married to Anna, and he lives in Kilmacolm, Scotland. They have two daughters and one son. He entered into full-time service in 1976 with the churches of God (www.churchesofgod.info). He has engaged in an itinerant ministry in western countries and has been privileged to serve the Lord in India and Myanmar (formerly Burma).

Other books written by Andy:

- Garments for Glory
- The Five Solas of the Reformation
- Grace in 1 Peter (Men God Moved - Volume 1)
- Boaz: Ruth's Bridegroom, Redeemer and Lord of the Harvest (Men God Moved - Volume 3)

ABOUT THE PUBLISHER

Hayes Press (www.hayespress.org) is a registered charity in the United Kingdom, whose primary mission is to disseminate the Word of God, mainly through literature. It is one of the largest distributors of gospel tracts and leaflets in the United Kingdom, with over 100 titles and many thousands despatched annually. In addition to paperbacks and eBooks, Hayes Press also publishes Plus Eagles Wings, a fun and educational Bible magazine for children, and Golden Bells, a popular daily Bible reading calendar in wall or desk formats.

If you would like to contact Hayes Press, there are a number of ways you can do so:

- By mail: c/o The Barn, Flaxlands, Royal Wootton Bassett, Wiltshire, UK SN4 8DY
- By phone: 01793 850598
- By eMail: info@hayespress.org
- via Facebook: www.facebook.com/hayespress.org

27429064R00076

Printed in Great Britain
by Amazon